PRAISES FOR

IN THE HEARTS OF HIS PEOPLE

"Laura Smith's, *In the Hearts of His People* is a fresh telling of the grand story of redemption, which unfolds in the Bible, from Genesis through Revelation. Laura's tender heart and the beautiful art combine, to tell the story with a special emphasis on the role of God's Holy Spirit in the history of redemption. Though written with children in mind, Laura's book will greatly encourage their parents as well."

—**Scotty Smith**, bestselling award winning author known for *Unveiled Hope* (with Michael Card), *Objects of His Affection, Restoring Broken Things* (with Steven Curtis Chapman), *Everyday Prayers: 365 Days to Gospel Centered Faith, and Every Season Prayers: Gospel-Centered Prayers for the Whole of Life.*

"*In the Hearts of His People* is a guided journey through the Bible...It fills the deep need of the next generation to engage with scripture."

—**Michael Card**, Christian Author, Singer/ Songwriter of 23 books and 30 albums. Michael is well known and loved through songs like *El Shaddai, Immanuel* and *Come Lift Up Your Sorrows.*

"An engaging and whimsically illustrated Story of all stories. Laura writes with heart and passion."

—**Diana Beach Batarseh**, creator of the popular *Ask Me WhoOo* series, The First Children's Catechism set to music word for word.

IN THE HEARTS OF HIS
PEOPLE

"GOD HAS SENT ME AND HIS SPIRIT." ISAIAH 48:16

LAURA SMITH
ILLUSTRATIONS BY OLIVIA SUSAN HANSON

NEW YORK

LONDON • NASHVILLE • MELBOURNE • VANCOUVER

IN THE HEARTS OF HIS PEOPLE

Published in New York, New York, by Morgan James Publishing. Morgan James is a trademark of Morgan James, LLC.
www.MorganJamesPublishing.com

The Morgan James Speakers Group can bring authors to your live event. For more information or to book an event visit The Morgan James Speakers Group at
www.TheMorganJamesSpeakersGroup.com.

ISBN 978-1-68350-715-4 paperback
ISBN 978-1-68350-716-1 eBook
Library of Congress Control Number: 2017912509

Cover & Interior Design by:
Megan Whitney
Creative Ninja Designs
megan@creativeninjadesigns.com

Original Cover Artwork Concept:
Julie Holt

In an effort to support local communities, raise awareness and funds,
Morgan James Publishing donates a percentage of all book sales for the life of each book to
Habitat for Humanity Peninsula and Greater Williamsburg.

Get involved today! Visit
www.MorganJamesBuilds.com

FOREWORD BY
DAVID CASSIDY

Imagine a child asking, "How does a tree sleep?"

That's a real question I was asked, and if you've spent any time with kids, I'm sure you've been asked some fun questions too! I laughed and was honest in my answer, "I don't know!"

We often struggle to answer children's questions…and that was an easy one because it's about our visible world! Rocks, clouds, oceans, fish, birds, and bugs are the subject of every child's hungry imagination and glorious curiosity.

But kids also ask questions about God. The often "simple and innocent" questions asked by children have challenged history's greatest thinkers. That's because these are questions about the mystical and invisible. If a visible tree is hard to explain, how can we communicate effectively with children when they ask about God?

Obviously, we start with Jesus: God made visible among us. Jesus as fully God and fully human has been described for over 2000 years. But what about when a child asks about the Holy Spirit: How do we talk about that invisible, amazingly powerful, presence? How do we describe the third person of the Trinity? And how do we help children understand that the Holy Spirit lives in our hearts today?

In the Hearts of His People is designed and written to help us more artfully talk about the mystery of the Holy Spirit to children. This colorful and friendly book helps children understand the big picture of the Spirit's work throughout the Bible. It helps us have something "concrete" to show our children about how God the Holy Spirit has been at work in creation and among his people all along—and will continue to do so as He works in each of our lives.

As you read this book to children, it is our hope and prayer that they will grow in their awareness that God is within them through the Holy Sprit. God will not only be the great and mighty God far above, He will also be more the God who is near to us and with us. This is so very important for every child to know (no matter how old they are!).

Will reading this book create more questions? Most likely the answer is yes! And that's a good thing. Remember, it's okay to say, "I don't know." Let those questions deepen your own study of Scripture and awaken your own childlike faith and curiosity as you seek answers for the precious little ones in your life.

May God the Holy Spirit, the agent of creation, the author of Scripture, guide you into His truth.

David Cassidy

Pastor, Christ Community Church

For more resources, go to www.LauraLangfordSmith.com.

DEDICATIONS

From Laura:
Dedicated with love to
Elizabeth, Wyatt, Chloe, Jeff, Virginia,
Beau, Macy, Molly, Finn, Mac,
Charlie, Belle, Cecelia, Otis, Otto, Mari, and Frederick.
And, in loving memory of Julie Holt and Stacey Brown.

From Olivia:
To Dad, who taught me the importance of reading the Scriptures
and applying them to the world around me;
to not follow what Society thinks is right,
but what God says is right.

To Mom, who gently steers me to think with my head
and not my heart;
to be sensible and level-headed.

To my brother, Ben,
who understands me
just because he is nearer my age.

To my brother, Calvin,
who helps stir up the flames of my imagination,
and keeps me exploring ever deeper.

To my little sister, Izzy,
who keeps the joy and laughter flowing.

Solo Deo Gloria.

ACKNOWLEDGEMENTS

There's an enormous number of friends and family I owe my deepest sincere thanks:

My husband, Geoff, for your continuous support, sacrifices and encouragement.

My mom, Linda; Father-in-law, Moose; daughter, Molly;
for your support and help in keeping the process going.

Karen Anderson, for believing in the concept and calling it "special." (I may never realize just how much you've done on my behalf to help make this book possible.) Thank you for your strategic mind, expert advice, and continuous love & prayers.

Rinda Smith, for pointing me in Karen's direction!

David Cassidy, for your Spirit-guided teaching on The Holy Spirit and inspiring the idea in the first place. Thank you for your insight and encouragement along the way, (though you were already drowning in work!)

Olivia, for your sweet and eager positive attitude, your dedication to the cause of glorifying The One and Only with these beautiful, fanciful illustrations—and of course, your putting up with me when I needed extra paintings or changes made.

Paul Colligan, for recommending Olivia!

Thank you to the Morgan James Team for taking this on, praying for this project, and your dedication in bringing it to its full potential.

Thank you to the many professional editors, teachers and theologians who've taken the time to give honest critiques and suggestions throughout the many stages of this book:

Anna Floit, Bob Lockhart, Kelly Thompson, Loral Robben Pepoon, Scotty Smith, Doris White, Cindy Najar, Lou Beasley, Joabe Andrade, Pat Toth, Melissa Shaw, Kay Dokkestul, Matthew & Roberta Creamer, Michael Card, Diana Beach Batarseh...

Thank you Phemie, Wendy, Suzanne, Li, Christina, Rachel, Laura, Claudia, Elizabeth, Beth—and everyone else who's prayed, encouraged, loved, and asked me for updates. (You know who you are.)

Most of all, I thank The Everlasting Father for all of your provisions in so many forms.

May this honor and glorify your name.

"But the fruit of the Spirit is love, joy, peace, patience, kindness, goodness, faithfulness, gentleness, self-control against such things there is no law."

(GALATIANS 5:22-23) ESV

May the God of hope fill you
with all joy and peace in believing,
so that by the power of the Holy Spirit
you may abound in hope.
(Romans 15:13) ESV

You will seek me and find me,
When you seek me with
all your heart.
(Jeremiah 29:13) ESV

Teach me to do your will,
for you are my God!
Let your good Spirit lead me on level ground!
(Psalms 143:10) ESV

IN THE BEGINNING, GOD

In the beginning, God creates the Heavens and the Earth through His Word.

In the beginning was the Word, and the Word was with God, and the Word was God. He was in the beginning with God. All things were made through him, and without him was not any thing made that was made. (John 1)

Darkness covers the face of the deep and The Spirit of God hovers over the waters.

Yet for us there is one God, the Father, from whom are all things and for whom we exist, and one Lord, Jesus Christ, through whom are all things and through whom we exist. (1 Corinthians 8:6)

God speaks
and...
Whoosh!...
His Spirit is sent like a wind breathing life and design into everything, everywhere!

The heavens declare the glory of God, and the sky above proclaims his handiwork.
Day to day pours out speech, and night to night reveals knowledge. There is no speech,
nor are there words, whose voice is not heard. (Psalms 19:1-3)

Out of the darkness,

He brings light.

Out of the dust,

He brings beauty.

In his hand is the life of every living thing and the breath of all mankind. (Job 12:10)

"Let us make man in our image,

after our likeness," God says.

"So God creates man in his own image,

in the image of God he creates him;

Male and female he creates them."

(Genesis 1:27)

He breathes into their nostrils

the breath of life,

and they become living,

thinking creatures.

The Lord God formed the man of dust from the ground and breathed into his nostrils the breath of life, and the man became a living creature. (Genesis 2:7)

Then God stops His work and rests in His perfect Holy place, delighting in His children. God wants His children to be in His presence forever with Him...flourishing in His garden and enjoying His good gifts.

The Spirit of God has made me, and the breath of the Almighty gives me life. (Job 33:4) NLT

He said to the woman, "Did God actually say, 'You shall not eat of any tree in the garden'...
You will not surely die. For God knows that when you eat of it your eyes will
be opened, and you will be like God..." (Genesis 3:2-5)

But after a while,

the first humans turn

away from God,

and a lie from God's

enemy echoes through

all human hearts for

ages to come...

a lie that says they don't need Him.

They cannot stay in His perfect resting place anymore.

A time of disorder, sickness, and death has begun.

He drove out the man, and at the east of the Garden of Eden he placed the cherubim and a flaming sword that turned every way to guard the way to the tree of life. (Genesis 3:24)

As hundreds of years go by,

the world becomes filthy.

Truth becomes mingled with lies.

There's meanness and madness and

bitterness and badness.

God's glorious good Spirit grieves.

Human hearts are only evil.

Then the Lord said, "My Spirit will not put up with humans for such a long time, for they are only mortal flesh. In the future, their normal lifespan will be no more than 120 years." (Genesis 6:3) NLT

None turn to God but one ...

a man named Noah.

Yet since the beginning, through all this evil,

our faithful Father had a plan ...

*The Lord saw that the wickedness of man was great in the earth, and that every intention
of the thoughts of his heart was only evil continually. (Genesis 6:5)*

God saves Noah and his family from a great flood

sent to wash away the growing evil in the world.

For almost all three seasons of summer, autumn, and winter,

they are safe inside of a giant ship, called an ark.

The ark begins to settle on a mountain tip appearing from the water.

For as were the days of Noah, so will be the coming of [Jesus] the Son of Man ... Therefore you also must be ready, for [Jesus] the Son of Man is coming at an hour you do not expect. (Matthew 24:37–44)

Noah opens the window and sends out a raven

to see if there is any dry ground.

The raven races across the waters,

finding nothing, yet, continues to hunt wearily ...

never returning to Noah and the refuge of the ark.

The waters increased and bore up the ark, and it rose high above the earth...Everything on the dry land in whose nostrils was the breath of life, died. (Genesis 7:17)

After seven days, the ark is still surrounded by water.

This time, Noah sends out a meek dove.

She glides to the North, East, South, and West across the waters.

But the dove found no place to set her foot, and she returned to him to the ark...So he put out his hand and took her and brought her into the ark with him. (Genesis 8:9)

Finding nowhere to set her foot, she circles back to shelter.

Noah holds out his hand and brings her inside to rest.

He waits seven more days...

You kept him in perfect peace whose mind is stayed on you, because he trusts in you. (Isaiah 26:3)

The ark is still surrounded by water.

He sends the dove out again.

Soon she is eagerly flitting through the air back toward the ark.

Noah's window is open to her. He holds out his hand and...

What's this? She's brought back a freshly plucked olive leaf!

What could this mean? She has found an olive tree!

The water must be receding!

"I will be like the dew to Israel; he shall blossom like the lily; he shall take root like the trees of Lebanon; his shoots shall spread out; his beauty shall be like the olive, and his fragrance like Lebanon.

So Noah waits seven more days and sends the dove out again. This time...

They shall return and dwell beneath my shadow; they shall flourish like the grain; they shall blossom like the vine; their fame shall be like the wine of Lebanon." (Hosea 14:5–7)

The dove finds a peaceful resting

place prepared especially for her.

Floodwaters go down and Earth has a fresh new start again.

"It was by faith Noah heard God's warnings about things that he could not yet see. He obeyed God and built a large boat to save his family. By his faith, Noah showed that the world was wrong. And he became one of those who are made right with God through faith." (Hebrews 11:7) ICB

"I establish my covenant with you, that never again shall all flesh be cut off by the waters of the flood, and never again shall there be a flood to destroy the earth...I have set my bow in the cloud, and it shall be a sign of the covenant between me and the earth." (Genesis 9:11-13).

Hundreds of years later, a man named Abraham is called by God.

God promises Abraham that through his only son,

he will have more children than there are stars in the sky and sands on Earth...

They will become a multitude of nations, and even kings will come from them!

"I swear by myself, declares the LORD, that because you have done this and have not withheld your son, your only son, I will surely bless you and make your descendants as numerous as the stars in the sky and as the sand on the seashore." (Genesis 22:16-17) NIV

And one day, through Abraham's own family, God will send a very special person.

In unity with God's Spirit, this very special person will do a wondrous thing...

He will be the way to unite God with His people again!

"Your father Abraham rejoiced as he looked forward to my coming. He saw it and was glad." ... Jesus answered, "I tell you the truth, before Abraham was even born, I AM!" (John 8:56, 58) NLT

GOD
SENDS HIS
SPIRIT

Many years later, God's family has grown in number.

God is ready, once again, to breathe the Word

And the patriarchs, jealous of Joseph, sold him into Egypt; but God was with him and rescued him out of all his afflictions and gave him favor and wisdom before Pharaoh...who made him ruler over Egypt and over all his household. Now there came a famine throughout all Egypt and Canaan, and great affliction, and our fathers could find no food. But when Jacob heard that there was grain in Egypt, he sent out our fathers on their first visit. And on the second visit Joseph made himself known to his brothers... (Acts 7:9-13)

and set His Spirit out on a very important mission.

First, He sends His Spirit upon a shepherd, named Joseph…

blessing him with gifts of interpretation and guidance.

And Pharaoh said to his servants, "Can we find a man like this, in whom is the Spirit of God?" (Genesis 41:38)

With His Spirit on Joseph, God holds out His hand and gathers His children under

His care so they would not die of hunger when famine falls upon the land.

So they sent a message to Joseph, saying, "Your father gave this command before he died: 'Say to Joseph,
"Please forgive the transgression of your brothers and their sin, because they did evil to you."' And now, please
forgive the transgression of the servants of the God of your father." Joseph wept when they spoke to him.

Not only does God save His own people, but He saves everyone else too! However, God's Spirit longs for a day when His resting place will be within the hearts of His people.

His brothers also came and fell down before him and said, "Behold, we are your servants." But Joseph said to them, "Do not fear, for am I in the place of God? As for you, you meant evil against me, but God meant it for good, to bring it about that many people should be kept alive..." (Genesis 50:16–20)

Four hundred years later, the number of
God's children has grown even larger than before.

*"I have surely seen the affliction of my people who are in Egypt, and) have heard their groaning,
and I have come down to deliver them." (Acts 7:34) God said to Moses, " I AM who I AM."
And he said, "Say this to the people of Israel: ' I AM has sent me to you.'" (Exodus 3:14)*

Yet, now they are in bondage, living under the threat of death.

So God sends His Spirit upon the meekest

man on Earth, named Moses...

fueling him with great faith.

*And Moses said to the people, "Fear not, stand firm, and see the salvation of the Lord,
which he will work for you today. For the Egyptians whom you see today, you shall never see again.
The Lord will fight for you, and you have only to be silent." (Exodus 14:13–14)*

guiding them toward

a homeland prepared

especially for them.

And The Spirit

patiently longs for the

day His resting place

will be in the hearts

of His people...

With His Spirit on Moses,

God holds out His hand

and makes a new way...

setting His children free

from slavery in a strange land.

As they follow,

they will not walk in darkness

but will have the light

of The Spirit...

"When Israel was a child, I loved him. And I called my son out of Egypt…it was I who taught Israel to walk. I took them by the arms. But they did not understand that I had healed them. I led them with cords of human kindness, with ties of love. I lifted the yoke from their neck. I bent down and fed them." (Hosea 11:1-4) ICB

With His Spirit on Moses in the wilderness,

God holds out His hand

and sprinkles down bread from heaven,

so the people will not hunger.

Then He strikes a rock,

bursting forth with a stream of flowing water,

so they will not thirst.

[Jesus said,] "Truly, truly, I say to you, it was not Moses who gave you the bread from heaven,
but my Father gives you the true bread from heaven. For the bread of God is he who comes
down from heaven and gives life to the world." (John 5-6:33)

And The Spirit patiently longs for the day His resting place will be in the hearts of His people.

And all ate the same spiritual food, and all drank the same spiritual drink. For they drank from the spiritual Rock that followed them, and the Rock was Christ. (1 Corinthians 10:3–4)

And he gave to Moses, when he had finished speaking with him on Mount Sinai, the two tablets of the testimony, tablets of stone, written with the finger of God. (Exodus 31:18)

With His Spirit on Moses in the wilderness, God holds out His finger

and writes His law on two stone tablets...

So His children can know how to live and love perfectly, without sin.

And The Spirit patiently longs for the day

His resting place will be in the hearts of His people.

*"I wish that all the LORD's people were prophets and that the LORD
would put his Spirit upon them all!" (Numbers 11:29) NLT*

God sends His Spirit upon a group of artists
blessed with skills of every craft.

*And beginning with Moses and all the Prophets, he [Jesus] interpreted to them in all the Scriptures
the things concerning himself... Then he said to them, "... everything written about me in the
Law of Moses and the Prophets and the Psalms must be fulfilled." (Luke 24:27-44)*

With His Spirit on the artists, God holds out His hand

and constructs a gorgeous golden treasure chest

called the Ark of the Covenant,

where they keep the tablets of His law.

Sealed with a mercy seat, topped by two shimmering angels,

the ark will be carried on their journey through wilderness and waters...

its precious treasure, hidden within.

*Let it be known to you...that through this man [Jesus] forgiveness of sins is proclaimed
to you, and by him everyone who believes is freed from everything from which you could not
be freed by the law of Moses. (Acts 13:38-39)*

With His Spirit on the artists,

God holds out His hand

and weaves together a beautiful, dazzling

tabernacle. Inside the tabernacle stands a

sacred room, veiled with walls of garden-designed

tapestry called The Most Holy Place...

where The Ark of the Covenant will rest.

"You shall command the people of Israel that they bring to you pure beaten olive oil for the light, that a lamp may regularly be set up to burn. In the tent of meeting, outside the veil that is before the testimony, Aaron and his sons shall tend it from evening to morning..." (Exodus 27:20-21)

And a pillar of The Spirit descends to
rest upon the tabernacle,
so the people can see God is with them.
But The Spirit longs for the day His resting
place will be in the hearts of His people.

The LORD replied, "My Presence will go with you, and I will give you rest." (Exodus 33:14) NIV

God sends His Spirit upon a young man named Joshua, blessed with leadership skills. With His Spirit on Joshua, God holds out His hand

If Joshua had given them rest, God would not have spoken of another day later on. So then, there remains a Sabbath rest for the people of God, for whoever has entered God's rest has also rested from his works as God did from his. Let us therefore strive to enter that rest... (Hebrews 4:8–11)

and safely leads His children to a land flowing with milk and honey...

A land prepared especially for them.

"And I will give you a new heart, and I will put a new spirit in you. I will take out your stony, stubborn heart and give you a tender, responsive heart."(Ezekiel 36:26) NLT

God sends His Spirit upon a good-hearted shepherd
named David—anointing him king. With His Spirit
on David, God holds out His hand
to protect His children and guide them in truth.

*Samuel took the horn of oil and anointed him in the midst of his brothers. And the Spirit of the Lord rushed
upon David... (1 Samuel 16:13) "Your word is a lamp to my feet and a light to my path." (Psalms 119:105)*

The Spirit inspires David with a bountiful bubbling of new songs in his heart... songs, glorifying God and His majestic name. And The Spirit longs for the day His resting place will be in the hearts of His people.

For he will hide me in his shelter in the day of trouble; he will conceal me under the cover of his tent; he will lift me high upon a rock ... and I will offer in his tent sacrifices with shouts of joy; I will sing and make melody to the Lord (Psalms 27:5–6)

God sends His Spirit upon King Solomon,

blessing him in all wisdom.

*"But will God really live on earth? Why, even the highest heavens cannot contain you.
How much less this Temple I have built!" (1 Kings 8:27)*

With His Spirit on Solomon, God holds out His hand

and builds a spectacular, magnificent temple...

and a cloud of The Spirit fills it up, overflowing with His glory.

But The Spirit still longs for the day His resting place will be in the hearts of His people.

"And it shall come to pass afterward, that I will pour out my Spirit on all flesh" (Joel 2:28)

Through all this time, the people try to obey God's law

to live and love perfectly,

but sadly, they aren't able to do it.

Hearts feel weary with a burdening guilt,

even though God cleanses them over and over again...

"Hear my cry for mercy as I call to you for help, as I lift up my hands toward your Most Holy Place." (Psalm 28:2) NIV
"Create in me a clean heart, O God, and renew a right spirit within me." (Psalm 51:12)
"I need someone to mediate between God and me, as a person mediates between friends." (Job 16:21) NLT

Many believe the old lie that they don't need God,

and they turn their backs on Him completely.

Filth and darkness creep up in the land and begin to take over...

leaving God's children scattered and distressed.

And so, The Spirit still longs for the day His

resting place will be in the hearts of His people.

"My people...have turned away from me. And I am the spring of living water. And they have dug their own wells. But they are broken wells that cannot hold water." (Jeremiah 2:13) ICB
"How often I have longed to gather your children together, as a hen gathers her chicks under her wings, and you were not willing." Matthew 23:37) NIV

GOD SENDS HIS SON

"Behold, I am doing a new thing;

now it springs forth,

do you not perceive it?

I will make a way in the

wilderness and rivers

in the desert."

(Isaiah 43:19)

When the time is right,

God sends His Spirit upon a young woman named Mary.

"And the angel answered her, 'The Holy Spirit will come upon you, and the power of the Most High will overshadow you; therefore the child to be born will be called holy—the Son of God.'" (Luke 1:35)

With His Spirit overshadowing Mary, God holds out His hand

and knits a very special baby inside her womb.

The baby grows inside Mary's tummy for three seasons,

when suddenly she feels quaking, aching labor pains...

*Therefore the Lord himself will give you a sign. Behold, the virgin shall conceive
and bear a son, and shall call his name Immanuel. (Isaiah 7:14)*

Mary's eyes well with tears as her heart swells with joy.

Then it happens. She sees baby Jesus appear at last...

The beautiful breath of heaven has become a human on Earth,

and He is placed into her

very own arms to rest.

"Draw near to me, hear this: from the beginning I have not spoken in secret, from the time it came to be I have been there." And now the Lord God has sent me, and his Spirit." (Isaiah 48:16)

The child will grow up strong in The Spirit, in wisdom,

truth, and might...and walk among His own creation;

His body, a true temple, filled up and overflowing with glory.

And one day...

And the Word ("logos") became flesh and dwelt ("tabernacled") among us, and we have seen his glory, glory as of the only Son from the Father, full of grace and truth. (John 1:14)

This very special man, Jesus, is surrounded by water. He rises up from the water, and behold, the heavens are open to Him.

The Spirit descends like a gentle dove to rest on Him... so the people can see God is with them. A voice from heaven says, "This is my beloved Son, with whom I am well pleased."

And he [John] preached, saying, "After me comes he who is mightier than I, the strap of whose sandals I am not worthy to stoop down and untie. I have baptized you with water, but he will baptize you with the Holy Spirit." (Mark 1:7–8)

You see, the same Spirit of God who hovered over the waters...

Who breathed life into every living thing... The same empowering Spirit

sent by The Father... Who gathered, freed, and fed His people...

Who gave them springs of water from the rock in a dry place...

The same Spirit... God's Holy Spirit...

had belonged to Jesus all along!

For the LORD your God is living among you. He is a mighty savior. He will take delight in you with gladness. With his love, he will calm all your fears. He will rejoice over you with joyful songs. (Zephaniah 3:17) NLT

Jesus holds out His hand, opens His mouth, and says,

"Let the little children come to me...

the kingdom of heaven belongs to such as these."

(Matthew 19:14) NIV

"Come to me, all you who are weary

and burdened, and I will give you rest.

Take my yoke upon you and learn from me,

for I am gentle and humble in heart,

and you will find rest for your souls."

(Matthew 11:30) NIV

The true light, which gives light to everyone, was coming into the world. He was in the world, and the world was made through him, yet the world did not know him." (John 1:9-10)

In Jesus, all the fullness of God was pleased to dwell. (Colossians 1:19)

"The Spirit of the LORD is upon me, for he has anointed me to bring
Good News to the poor. He has sent me to proclaim

"I AM the light of the world.

Whoever follows me will not walk in darkness,

but will have the light of life."

(John 8:12)

that captives will be released, that the blind will see,
that the oppressed will be set free," (Luke 4:18) NLT

"I AM the bread of life; whoever comes to me shall not hunger, and whoever believes in me shall never thirst."

(John 6:35)

"If anyone thirsts, let him come to me and drink. Whoever believes in me, as the Scripture has said, 'Out of his heart will flow rivers of living water.'"

Now this he said about the Spirit, whom those who believed in him were to receive, for as yet the Spirit had not been given, because Jesus was not yet glorified. (John 7:37–39)

"I AM the good shepherd.

The good shepherd lays down his life for the sheep."

(John 10:11)

The Lord is my shepherd. I have everything I need. He gives me rest in green pastures. He leads me to calm water. He gives me new strength. For the good of his name, he leads me on paths that are right. Even if I walk through a very dark valley, I will not be afraid because you are with me.

"[My sheep hear my voice and I know them...

they will follow me...

Your rod and your shepherd's staff comfort me. You prepare a meal for me in front of my enemies. You pour oil of blessing on my head. You give me more than I can hold. Surely your goodness and love will be with me all my life. And I will live in the house of the Lord forever. (Psalms 23:1-6) ICB

I will give them a forever life...

so they will never die.

Jesus answered, "Truly, truly, I say to you, unless one is born of water and the Spirit, he cannot enter the kingdom of God. That which is born of the flesh is flesh, and that which is born of the Spirit is spirit. Do not marvel that I said to you, 'You must be born again.'

I and the Father are one]."

(John 10:27-28)

The wind blows where it wishes, and you hear its sound, but you do not know where it comes from or where it goes. So it is with everyone who is born of the Spirit." (John 3:5-8)

Jesus holds out His hand and makes the blind to see, the deaf to hear,

"I am the resurrection and the life. Whoever believes in me, though he die, yet shall he live,

and the lame to leap like a deer.

He heals the sick, raises the dead, and makes the muted sing for joy!

Then one day, He explains...

and everyone who lives and believes in me shall never die. Do you believe this?" (John 11:25–26)

"[I must go to my Father.

If I do not go away, my Spirit will not come to rest in you.

My Father will send Him as your helper, comforter,

and counselor... He will show you the truth about me.

If you know me, then you know the Father also.

You have seen Him.

He took some bread and gave thanks to God for it. Then he broke it in pieces and gave it to the disciples, saying, "This is my body, which is given for you. Do this in remembrance of me." After supper he took another cup of wine and said, "This cup is the new covenant between God and his people—an agreement confirmed with my blood, which is poured out as a sacrifice for you." (Luke 22:19-20) NLT

My Father's house has many rooms,

and I am going back to prepare a place, especially for you.

I will come again and take you to myself.

You know the way to where I am going.

I am the way, and the truth, and the life.

No one comes to the Father except through Me.]"

(John 14)

God made Christ, who never sinned, to be the offering for our sin, so that we could be made right with God through Christ. (2 Corinthians 5:21) NLT

The Father loves His children so very much,

that He came through His Spirit and only Son,

to become the new way back to Him.

GARDEN
OF
GETHSEMANE
·OLIVE PRESS·

Because God's children are human beings—made of flesh and blood—the Son also became flesh and blood.
For only as a human being could he die, and only by dying could he break the power...of death.

Because of what Jesus would do next,

to wash away the sins of His children once and for all...

Only in this way could he set free all who have lived their lives as slaves to the fear of dying...
Then he could offer a sacrifice that would take away the sins of the people. (Hebrews 2:14-17) NLT

Taking the punishment of sin for us...

He was bruised for our iniquities: the chastisement of our peace was upon him; and with his stripes we are healed. All we like sheep have gone astray; we have turned every one to his own way; and the Lord hath laid on him the iniquity of us all. (Isaiah 53:5-6) KJV

For, There is one God and one Mediator who can reconcile God and humanity—the man Christ Jesus. He gave his life to purchase freedom for everyone. This is the message God gave to the world at just the right time. (1 Timothy 2:5-6) NLT

And since Jesus conquered death and was raised back to life,

we are free to have a fresh, clean start again, as new creations...

free to serve in love, without any fear of death.

Because of Jesus, God's people can have the

gift of His Spirit living with us, upon us, and

inside of us, filling us up.

And she saw two angels in white, sitting where the body of Jesus had lain, one at the head and one at the feet. (John 20:12) And he said to them, "Do not be alarmed. You seek Jesus of Nazareth, who was crucified. He has risen; he is not here." (Mark 16:6)

*And when he [Jesus] had said this, he breathed on them and said to them,
"Receive the Holy Spirit." (John 20:22) "If anyone belongs to Christ, then he is made new.
The old things have gone; everything is made new!" (2 Corinthians 5:17) ICB*

"If anyone loves me, he will keep my word, and my Father will love him, and we will come to him and make our home with him...But the Helper, the Holy Spirit, whom the Father will send in my name, he will teach you all things and bring to your remembrance all that I have said to you. Peace I leave with you; my peace I give to you..." (John 14:23-27)

When we have The Holy Spirit through Christ, we will never be alone.

He is always within us like treasure in our hearts,

and the guiding light as we journey to share the good news...

until the day He calls us home to the place He prepares especially for us.

Suddenly a sound like the blowing of a violent wind came from heaven and filled the whole house where they were sitting. They saw what seemed to be tongues of fire that separated and came to rest on each of them. All of them were filled with the Holy Spirit... (Acts 2:2-4) NIV

Through Jesus and His Spirit, God holds out His hand and builds a kingdom with a multitude of living stones that no one could number. From every nation, language, and tribe,

I heard a loud shout from the throne, saying, "Look, God's home is now among his people! He will live with them, and they will be his people. God himself will be with them. He will wipe every tear from their eyes, and there will be no more death or sorrow or crying or pain. All these things are gone forever."

The Spirit wraps around each one...

So we may stand before the throne of God, as innocent as Jesus...

and enter, finally, into His Sabbath rest, forever.

And the one sitting on the throne said, "Look, I am making everything new!" And then he said to me, "Write this down, for what I tell you is trustworthy and true...It is finished! I am the Alpha and the Omega— the Beginning and the End. To all who are thirsty I will give freely from the springs of the water of life. All who are victorious will inherit all these blessings, and I will be their God, and they will be my children." (Revelation 21:3-7) NLT

VERSES & QUOTES

And you also were included in Christ when you heard the message of truth, the gospel of your salvation. When you believed, you were marked in him with a seal, the promised Holy Spirit, who is a deposit guaranteeing our inheritance until the redemption of those who are God's possession —to the praise of his glory.
(Ephesians 1:13-14) NIV

Or do you not know that your body is a temple of the Holy Spirit within you, whom you have from God? You are not your own, for you were bought with a price. So glorify God in your body.
(1 Corinthians 6:19-20)

Holiness, as taught in the Scriptures, is not based upon knowledge on our part. Rather, it is based upon the resurrected Christ in-dwelling us and changing us into His likeness."
(A.W. Tozer)

After creation God said, 'It is finished' and he rested.
After redemption Jesus said, 'It is finished' and we can rest.
(Timothy Keller)

Without the Spirit we can neither love God nor keep His commandments.
(Augustine)

Those in whom the Spirit comes to live are God's new Temple.
They are, individually and corporately, places where heaven and earth meet.
(N.T. Wright)

The Holy Spirit illuminates the minds of people, makes us yearn for God,
and takes spiritual truth and makes it understandable to us.
(Billy Graham)

For you have been called to live in freedom, my brothers and sisters.
But don't use your freedom to satisfy your sinful nature.
Instead, use your freedom to serve one another in love.
For the whole law can be summed up in this one command:
"Love your neighbor as yourself."...So I say, let the Holy Spirit
guide your lives. Then you won't be doing what your sinful nature craves...
But when you are directed by the Spirit, you are not under obligation to the law of Moses.
(Galatians 5:13-18) NLT

The Holy Spirit is not in a hurry. Character is the produce of a lifetime.
(John Stott)

Trying to do the Lord's work in your own strength is the most
confusing, exhausting, and tedious of all work.
But when you are filled with the Holy Spirit, then the
ministry of Jesus just flows out of you.
(Corrie Ten Boom)

The Spirit is the first power we practically experience,
but the last power we come to understand.
(Oswald Chambers)

For I can do everything through Christ, who gives me strength.
(Philippians 4:13) NLT

For all creation is waiting eagerly for that future day
when God will reveal who His children really are.
Against its will, all creation was subjected to God's curse.
But with eager hope, the creation looks forward to the day when it will
join God's children in glorious freedom from death and decay.

For we know that all creation has been groaning as in the
pains of childbirth right up to the present time.

And we believers also groan, even though we have the
Holy Spirit within us as a foretaste of future glory, for we long
for our bodies to be released from sin and suffering.

We, too, wait with eager hope for the day when God will give us our
full rights as His adopted children, including the new bodies He has promised us.
We were given this hope when we were saved...

And the Holy Spirit helps us in our weakness.
For example, we don't know what God wants us to pray for.
But the Holy Spirit prays for us with groanings that cannot be expressed in words.

And the Father who knows all hearts knows what the Spirit is saying,
for the Spirit pleads for us believers in harmony with God's own will.

And we know that God causes everything to work together for the good of those
who love God and are called according to His purpose for them.
(Romans 8:18-28) NLT

ABOUT THE AUTHOR

Laura Langford Smith is a stay-at-home mom with a background of studies in English, children's literature, journalism, and creative writing.

Laura has been serving in church children's ministry for over ten years in the Nashville area, with four of those years volunteering as the children's ministry director/teacher for a young international church plant.

She's been married to her husband, Geoff, for nearly 17 years and they have a daughter and son, ages 15 and nearly 7. Laura enjoys arts, crafts, cooking, gardening, sewing, and reading with her children.

ABOUT THE ILLUSTRATOR

This is Olivia Susan Hanson's first illustrated book. She is a self-taught artist and has loved painting and sketching from a very young age, winning her first art competition at the age of 4.

She graduated from Cor Deo Christian Academy in 2016, where her father is the principal.

The oldest of 4 children, Olivia lives on a farm in Hillsboro, Oregon and enjoys long country walks, reading classic literature, and drinking Kombucha. While merely eighteen years old, Olivia painted all illustrations by hand. You can see more of her artwork on Instagram @oliviasusanhanson.

Printed in the USA
CPSIA information can be obtained
at www.ICGtesting.com
JSHW072020140824
68134JS00041B/3719

9 781683 507154

USA
SOCCER

DON GULBRANDSEN

TRIUMPH
BOOKS

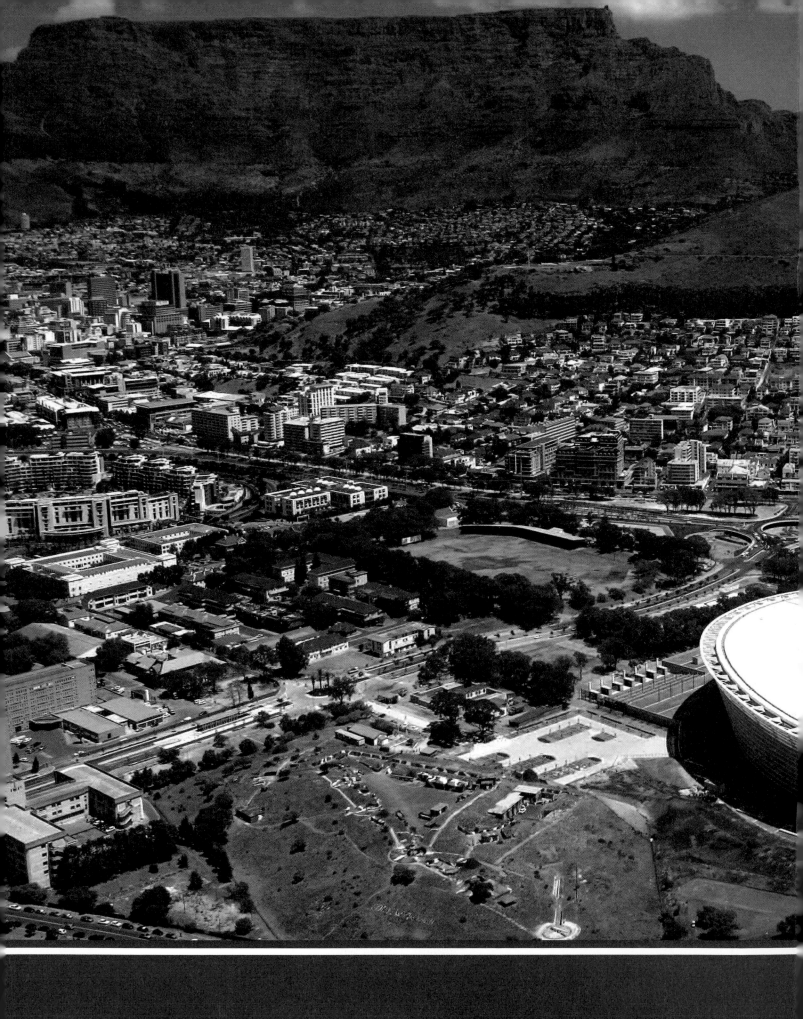

Though Cape Town's brand-new Green Point Stadium is part of a beautiful South African scene, come June 2010 it will be a field of battle for several World Cup matches.

This book is available in quantity at special discounts for your group or organization. For further information contact:

Triumph Books
542 South Dearborn Street
Suite 750
Chicago, IL 60605
Phone: (312) 939-3330
Fax: (312) 663-3557
www.triumphbooks.com

Printed in the United States of America
ISBN: 978-1-60078-302-9

All photographs courtesy of Getty Images except where otherwise noted.

Content packaged by Mojo Media, Inc.
Joe Funk: Editor
Jason Hinman: Creative Director

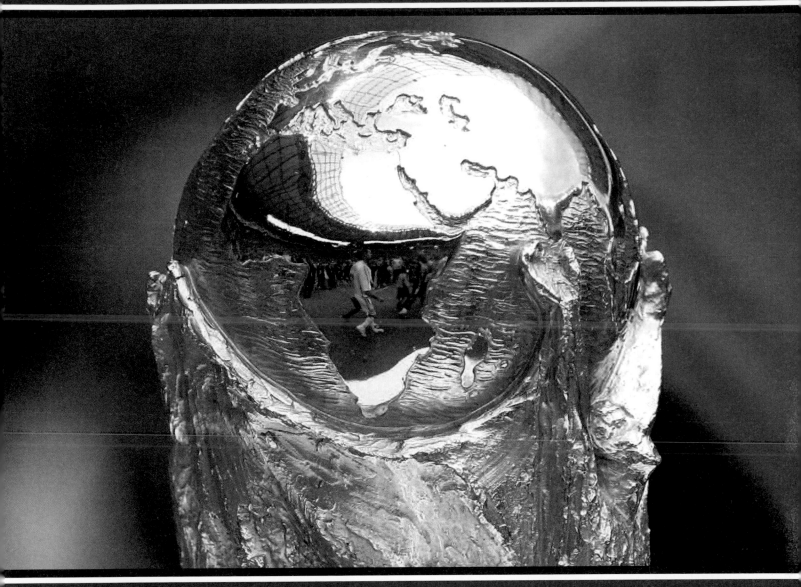

contents

Introduction

As 2010 dawned, excitement for the year's World Cup finals, scheduled to commence in June in South Africa, was building around the world. Fans from 32 nations—some perennial powers and some rare entrants in the tournament—all harbored dreams of victory...if not in the tournament final, then at least in a key game or two or three, a result that would prove their country's worthiness of competing on the soccer world's biggest stage.

In the United States, the level of obsession with the world's biggest soccer tournament may be modest compared to other countries, but don't doubt for a minute that many, many people can't wait for play to begin. This is a wonderful time to be a fan of the United States Men's National Team—it is truly the squad's golden era. The U.S. has qualified for six straight World Cups, reaching the quarterfinals in 2002. The team's player pool is punctuated by names found on the rosters of top-division European club teams as well as the All-Stars of Major League Soccer. And this is a team whose excellence has spanned generations and promises more success in the future thanks to an effective talent-development program.

And then there is the team's recent performance. If 2009 was any indication, 2010 could be a historic year for the United States Men's National Team.

The U.S. quest for a spot in the 2010 World Cup began in earnest on a wet February 2009 night in Ohio. Opening the final CONCACAF qualifying round against rival Mexico at Columbus Crew Stadium, the U.S. team was greeted by a sellout crowd and an electric atmosphere. After 90 minutes of nearly flawless play, the Americans had soundly defeated the Mexicans, 2–0, and looked destined to stroll to a berth in South Africa. If only things had ended up being that easy.

Though the Americans maintained a grip on the top spot in the CONCACAF region right through the final game in October—a shaky 2–2 draw against Costa Rica—the year was a crazy roller-coaster ride for the U.S. team. Easy victories were counterbalanced by frustrating losses, new stars emerged only to be felled by heartbreaking injuries, and confident performances were followed by lackluster ones. As 2009 progressed, fans couldn't help but ask, "How good *is* this team?"

The answer came in late June. The U.S. team, as defending champion of the previous year's CONCACAF Gold Cup, was invited to participate in the prestigious Confederations Cup tournament. Though the United States seemed destined to be one of the CONCACAF qualifiers for the 2010 finals,

Clint Dempsey is on cloud nine as he celebrates the opening goal of the 2010 Confederations Cup final against Brazil. The score off a Jonathan Spector cross was Dempsey's third in three games.

the World Cup warm-up in South Africa offered an opportunity to see how well the team could perform against some of the planet's top squads. Things didn't start well. Thrown immediately into the fray against Italy and Brazil, the Americans bombed, losing by a combined score of 6–1. There were rumbles that coach Bob Bradley's job was on the line. Fans started to dread the 2010 World Cup, expecting results similar to what the disappointing 1998 and 2006 teams posted.

Yet this tournament ended up proving that 2006 was ancient history. This *new* American team had several things going for it. Holdover stars from the previous World Cup, including Landon Donovan, Clint Dempsey, Oguchi Onyewu, and Carlos Bocanegra, were still at the top of their

game. In addition, new talents had emerged: goalkeeper Tim Howard, midfielder Michael Bradley, striker Jozy Altidore, and others. And the ever-calm Bob Bradley, not necessarily the first choice to be the American head coach, had nonetheless instilled in his squad a quiet confidence that reflected his own personality.

So with their backs against the wall at the Confederations Cup, an amazing thing happened to the American men: they refused to panic. Instead, they relaxed, regrouped, and played with energy...and made a miracle happen by beating Egypt 3–0 to stay in the tournament. They followed up this outstanding performance with an even better one—beating Spain, the world's top-ranked team and the early World Cup favorite, in the

Seen here training before a match in El Salvador, the United States Men's National Team experienced plenty of turnover between the 2006 and 2010 World Cups, though several of the biggest names still lead the team.

semifinal, 2–0. It might have been the best game ever played by the U.S. men's team.

Though the U.S. lost the tournament final to Brazil (putting on yet another strong performance), the victory over Spain changed everything. The U.S. press, which rarely covers soccer, took notice and started to talk about the team. American soccer fans, in somewhat of a funk since the 2006 World Cup, were reinvigorated, thinking that—maybe—their team had a chance to win it all. And the world took notice. After their loss, Spanish players insisted that the U.S. win was a fluke, something that couldn't be repeated...yet the looks on their faces revealed a different message. There was a sense that Spain would prefer not having to play the U.S. come World Cup time.

After the Confederations Cup, the U.S. team proceeded confidently through its remaining CONCACAF qualifying games and secured the top spot in the region. Though their performances weren't always pretty, you could sense something different about the team, a never-say-die attitude that typically only shows itself in teams that truly believe they can win every game they play—no matter how little time is left and how many goals they are behind. If the U.S. can maintain this attitude and deliver a performance that truly reflects its collective talents, the 2010 World Cup could end up being a highly entertaining tournament for American soccer fans.

Head coach Bob Bradley looks concerned as he leaves the field following the challenging first half of the United States' qualifying game against Honduras.

Facing a tough Mexico squad and more than 100,000 hostile fans at Estadio Azteca, Carlos Bocanegra and Oguchi Onyewu get airborne to battle for the ball during Team USA's August 2009 qualifier in Mexico City.

From CONCACAF to SOUTH AFRICA

Qualifying for the one of the 32 precious slots in the quadrennial World Cup finals is better described as a marathon than a sprint. In some regions, the qualifying rounds seem to go on forever. In South America, for example, the 10 nations competing for four guaranteed spots (plus the opportunity to play into the tournament for a fifth team) in the ultracompetitive region play 18 games over a two-year period. The qualifying "league" wraps up play in October prior to the following year's Cup. Nearly three years elapse from the start of qualifying for the South American teams until the top clubs finally appear in the tournament.

In professional sports, three years can be an eternity, and it is rare when a national soccer team maintains continuity throughout that period. Established stars age and fall out of favor, injuries take their toll, young new stars emerge, and managers are changed. The clubs that best adapt to the inevitable change and maintain their excellence throughout qualifying fare the best—a spot in the finals is almost always well earned.

Where do the teams come from?

Teams from 32 countries qualified for the 2010 World Cup finals in South Africa. One team qualified automatically: the host nation, South Africa. The other participants are drawn from the six regions around the globe: South America, four automatic qualifiers; Europe, 13 automatic qualifiers; Africa, five qualifiers in addition to the host nation; CONCACAF (North America, Central America, Caribbean), three automatic qualifiers; and Asia, four automatic qualifiers. The final region, Oceania, does not receive an automatic bid, but the winner of the group gets the opportunity to play the fifth-place Asian squad for a spot in the finals. The final slot in South Africa goes to the winner of a playoff between the fourth-place CONCACAF team and the fifth-place South American team.

Goalkeeper Tim Howard, teammates, and fans celebrate after the October 2009 draw against Costa Rica in Washington, D.C., guaranteed the United States first place in the CONCACAF qualifying region.

All About CONCACAF

The United States calls CONCACAF—shorthand for the Confederation of North, Central America, and Caribbean Association Football—its home for FIFA-sanctioned soccer. The organization has been around since 1961 and recognizes 40 members. Of those, only 35 are approved for play in FIFA events, and that is the group that takes part in the playoff for the three precious automatic slots in the World Cup finals.

To describe CONCACAF as an unusual region is an understatement. Most of the nations are better known as vacation destinations than as soccer powerhouses, and in fact a significant number of the members are tiny island nations with relatively small populations. Not surprisingly, the two most populous countries, the United States and Mexico, have dominated in terms of the number of World Cup final appearances. Mexico leads the list with 13 appearances, followed by the United States with eight, Cost Rica with three, El Salvador with two, and Canada, Cuba, Haiti, Honduras, Jamaica, and Trinidad & Tobago with one apiece.

In addition to World Cup qualifying (for both men and women), CONCACAF oversees a number of soccer events in this part of the world, including the CONCACAF Champions League for professional clubs and the biennial CONCACAF Gold Cup tournament, which is open to all 40 members in the region.

CONCACAF World Cup Qualifying

Winnowing 35 teams down to three automatic qualifiers and a fourth playoff qualifier is not a simple process and takes nearly two years to complete. The latest CONCACAF qualifying tournament started in February 2008 and wrapped up in mid-October 2009.

Four rounds comprise the qualifying process. The 13 highest-rated

CONCACAF World Cup Qualifying Pool

- Anguilla
- Antigua and Barbuda
- Aruba
- Bahamas
- Barbados
- Belize
- Bermuda
- British Virgin Islands
- Canada
- Cayman Islands
- Costa Rica
- Cuba
- Dominica
- Dominican Republic
- El Salvador
- Grenada
- Guatemala
- Guyana
- Haiti
- Honduras
- Jamaica
- Mexico
- Montserrat
- Netherlands Antilles
- Nicaragua
- Panama
- Puerto Rico
- St. Kitts and Nevis
- St. Lucia
- St. Vincent and Grenadines
- Suriname
- Trinidad & Tobago
- Turks and Caicos Islands
- U.S. Virgin Islands
- United States

With many small fish—like Haiti, with just 11 million residents—in the CONCACAF pond, it's not surprising that the U.S. (represented here by Stuart Holden) and Mexico dominate the region.

teams (as determined by FIFA's rankings) are given a bye in the first round, while the remaining 22 teams are paired up for a home-and-away series with the 11 winners advancing to the second round on aggregate goals. (In the latest qualifying, three of these series were limited to a single game because one of the teams involved lacked a FIFA-approved stadium. Other ties saw games played at neutral sites, and one matchup saw both games in one location. Quality stadiums are definitely lacking among CONCACAF teams.)

The second round repeats the home-and-away, aggregate-goal format with teams ranked 1–12 randomly paired against teams ranked 13–24. The 12 winners move on to the third round, where they are placed in three groups of four teams. Every team plays the other three in their group both at home and away. At the end of this mini-league, the top two finishers in each group progress to the final round—known in CONCACAF as the Hexagonal, for its six participants.

The Hexagonal runs from February through October in the year prior to the World Cup finals. Like the third round, every club plays the other five teams both home and away. The top three finishers on points (with ties broken by goal differential) after this 10-game schedule earn automatic Cup final bids. The fourth-place team gets a second chance in the form of a playoff against the number-five South American team.

This format is no cakewalk. Staying on task for 18 games (or 20 for teams that have to play in the first round) requires more than just talent; resilience and at least a little luck are also helpful. And while CONCACAF squads aren't frequently mentioned among the world's best, they produce many talented players capable of playing professionally in the world's best league. They also possess a secret weapon: home-field advantage.

CONCACAF counts among its members some of the most challenging and intimidating venues for playing soccer...especially if you're a visiting player. Rabid fans are part of the problem; when they aren't screaming (nonstop) they are hurling coins, batteries, or cups full of beer or other unmentionable fluids at opposing players. Referees are often noticeably affected by the open or implied threats to their lives offered by fans, and it becomes difficult for visiting teams to get a fair shake on close calls. There is also the physical environment to consider. In some countries, the quality of the stadium and/or pitch leaves something to be desired and gives the home team, familiar with the poor conditions, a marked advantage. Cost Rica and its infamous artificial-turf field is a prime example of this. Aztec Stadium in Mexico City offers another challenge. The city's high altitude and horrendous air pollution provide a double whammy that can bring a poorly acclimated player to his knees long before the final whistle.

As is usually the case, goalkeeping was a strong suit for the United States throughout World Cup qualifying. There are a number of elite keepers that hail from the United States, with Tim Howard leading the way.

CONCACAF Fourth-Round (Hexagonal) Final Standings

	W	L	D	GS	GA	GD	Pts
Q: United States	6	2	2	19	13	+6	20
Q: Mexico	6	3	1	18	12	+6	19
Q: Honduras	5	4	1	17	11	+6	16
P: Costa Rica	5	4	1	15	15	0	16
El Salvador	2	6	2	9	15	-6	8
Trinidad & Tobago	1	6	3	10	22	-12	6

Q: Qualified for 2010 World Cup   **P**: Qualified for playoff with Uruguay (South America)

The U.S. Journey through CONCACAF

The United States entered the CONCACAF qualifying for the 2010 World Cup as the second-highest-ranked team in the region (Mexico was the highest-ranked club) and earned a bye through the first round. In the second round, the U.S. drew Barbados, the 14th seed entering the competition and thus the highest-seeded team not to draw a first-round bye. Barbados had earned its pass to the next round thanks to a hard-fought 2–1 aggregate victory over 28th-seeded Dominica. Surprisingly, the Barbadians did not put up much of a fight, and the United States notched an 8–0 rout in their June 15, 2008, tie in Carson, California. The U.S. coasted to a 1–0 win in Barbardos one week later, moving to Round 3 with a 9–0 aggregate.

In Round 3, the Americans were grouped Trinidad & Tobago, Guatemala, and Cuba for their August-November 2008 mini-league. The U.S. established its superiority quickly, winning their first four games (over Guatemala 1–0, Cuba 1–0, Trinidad & Tobago 3–0, and Cuba 6–1) to clinch advancement to the final round. For the final two games, coach Bob Bradley had the luxury of giving generous field time to inexperienced players, and the results were fairly positive: a narrow 2–1 loss to Trinidad & Tobago (thanks to a late penalty) and a 2–0 win over Guatemala.

Thanks to its solid play, the United States had earned the right to move on to the Hexagonal. Despite its berth in CONCACAF's final qualifying round, there were still lingering questions about the team, which had been under intense scrutiny since its disappointing performance at World Cup 2006 in Germany. Despite a relatively deep and talented pool of players to pick from, Bob Bradley still didn't seem to have a regular lineup in place. And while the team was capable of brilliance at times, it was equally capable of looking completely overmatched, even by much lesser squads. Entering the Hexagonal, qualification for the World Cup final was anything but assured, especially with five solid teams to contend with. And the first matchup for the final round, scheduled for February 11, 2009, in Columbus, Ohio, was archrival Mexico. The U.S. team needed to figure out exactly who they were—and quickly.

CONCACAF
Hexagonal Team Capsules

United States of America
Population 2009: 305 million
Capital: Washington,
District of Columbia
Nickname: Red, White, and Blue
FIFA World Cups Hosted (1): 1994
Previous World Cup Appearances (8): 1930,
1934, 1950, 1990, 1994, 1998, 2002, 2006
Top Finish: 3rd place, 1934
Most-Capped Player (164): Cobi Jones,
1992–2004
Most Goals (41): Landon Donovan, 2000–

Mexico
Population 2009: 111 million
Capital: Mexico City
Nickname: El Tri (Tricolores)
FIFA World Cups Hosted (2): 1970, 1986
Previous World Cup Appearances (13): 1930,
1950, 1954, 1958, 1962, 1966, 1970, 1978,
1986, 1994, 1998, 2002, 2006
Top Finish: Quarterfinals, 1970 and 1986
Most-Capped Player (178): Claudio Suarez,
1992–2006
Most Goals (46): Jared Borgetti, 1997–

Honduras
Population: 7.8 million
Capital: Tegucigalpa
Nickname: Los Catrachos
Previous World Cup Appearances (1): 1982
Top Finish: Round 1, 1982
Most-Capped Player (127): Arnado Guevara, 1994–
Most Goals (55): Carlos Pavon, 1993–

El Salvador
Population: 7.1 million
Capital: San Salvador
Nickname: La Selecta
Previous World Cup Appearances (2): 1970, 1982
Top Finish: Round 1, 1970 and 1982
Most-Capped Player (89): Luis Guevara Mora,
1979–1996
Most Goals (41): Jorge "Magico" Gonzalez,
1979–1998

Costa Rica
Population: 4.5 million
Capital: San Jose
Nickname: Los Ticos
Previous World Cup Appearances (3): 1990,
2002, 2006
Top Finish: Round 2, 1990
Most-Capped Player (131): Walter Centeno, 1995–
Most Goals (47): Rolando Fonseca, 1992–

Trinidad & Tobago
Population: 1.2 million
Capital: Port of Spain
Nickname: Soca Warriors
Previous World Cup Appearances (1): 2006
Top Finish: Round 1, 2006
Most-Capped Player (117): Angus Eve, 1994–2005
Most Goals (69): Stern John, 1995–

CONCACAF
Final Round: U.S. Game Capsules

United States 2, Mexico 0

February 11, 2009

Columbus Crew Stadium, Columbus, Ohio

Attendance: 23,776

The U.S. brain trust probably thought that scheduling a winter game in a northern location would give the Americans a weather advantage over the visitors from Mexico. The weather was a factor, but not in the way everyone expected. Temperatures were relatively mild (in the 50s), but torrential rain shortly before kickoff threatened to turn the pitch into a quagmire. Despite the soggy conditions, the atmosphere was electric—typical of every contest between the Stars and Stripes and Tricolores—though recent results indicate the U.S. has turned this rivalry into a one-sided affair north of the border.

As the whistle blew and the game unfolded, it quickly became apparent that these were two teams functioning on different planes. Mexico, as always, was blessed with an impressive collection of soccer talent, but it was not the same unified collection that it had been in the past. Playing under the cloud of a managerial controversy— stoic Swede Sven-Goran Eriksson's job apparently in jeopardy—Mexico had been struggling to find its identity as a team.

Starting what would become a distressing trend in this qualifying round, an early U.S. gaffe nearly led to a Mexico goal in the third minute, but Tim Howard thwarted a chance for Giovani Dos Santos, the first of many confident plays for the talented keeper. After that early defensive slip, the Americans asserted control with crisp passing and relentless pressure that had the Mexicans scrambling. The Americans finally broke through just before the half. DeMarcus Beasley's corner found Landon Donovan on the far post. He smartly headed back into the center to Oguchi Onyewu, who used his own head to direct a sharp shot on goal. Mexican keeper Oswaldo Sanchez parried the shot, but Michael Bradley sent the rebound into the back of the net for the 1–0 halftime lead.

The Mexicans made a better start of the second half and Dos Santos nearly equalized in the 65th minute when, suddenly, everything unraveled for the Tricolores. Rafael Marquez made a vicious spikes-up challenge on Howard that drew a red card. With the 11-on-10 advantage, the United States cruised to a relatively easy victory. Michael Bradley capped the win with an injury-time goal initiated by Jozy Altidore, with Landon Donovan again providing the key link in the scoring play.

The 2–0 win gave the U.S. its 11th straight home game against Mexico without a loss and, for the time being, the top spot in the Hexagonal.

Landon Donovan fights through a physical challenge to get to a loose ball. Though he didn't score either United States goal in the 2–0 win over Mexico, he was instrumental in setting up both tallies.

United States 2, El Salvador 2

March 28, 2009

Estadio Cuscatlan, San Salvador, El Salvador

Attendance: 30,350

All the good feelings generated by February's 2–0 victory over Mexico quickly disappeared when the United States traveled to El Salvador for its first away match in the CONCACAF Hexagonal. Despite a rowdy partisan crowd, the Americans looked solid in the opening minutes until an error by DaMarcus Beasley led to a Salvadoran counterattack that culminated in an Eliseo Quintanilla goal in the 15th minute. After conceding that first goal, U.S. second-choice goalkeeper Brad Guzan kept the U.S. in the game with some solid work, but the Americans couldn't muster much offense to support him.

In the second half Bob Bradley brought in Jozy Altidore and Jose Francisco Torres as offensive-minded subs, moving Beasley back on defense—but the move soon backfired. Beasley conceded a cross that Cristian Castillo headed into the goal for a 2–0 lead in the 72nd minute. With things looking desperate, the United States finally notched up the offensive pressure, scoring just five minutes later when a perfect Frankie Hedjuk cross was deftly headed into the net by Altidore. The Americans continued to press and were rewarded with the tying goal—from a Hedjuk header on a corner kick—and a hard-earned point that kept them in first place in the Hexagonal.

In a close game, El Salvador's Alfredo Pacheco grabs Clint Dempsey's jersey as the two players vie for the ball during the March 2009 qualifier in San Salvador.

United States 3, Trinidad & Tobago 0
April 1, 2009
LP Field, Nashville, Tennessee,
Attendance: 27,959

After the nail-biter in El Salvador, the U.S. Men's National Team enjoyed a little home cooking in Tennessee, recording a confidence-building shutout over Trinidad & Tobago. The game will probably be looked back on as the coming-out party for talented young striker Jozy Altidore. After Altidore jump-started the dramatic come-from-behind draw with El Salvador just a few days earlier, Bob Bradley inserted him in the starting lineup against T&T. Altidore rewarded the head coach for his decision by recording a spectacular hat trick in the easy victory.

In addition to Bradley, Altidore had Landon Donovan to thank for his trio of goals. The American captain provided the assist on all three tallies. The first score came in just the 13th minute after a nice exchange between Brian Ching and Donovan led to a cross that found Altidore in position to convert. That goal would have been enough for the win because T&T put just a single shot on goal (easily saved by Tim Howard) all game. Nonetheless, Altidore sealed the win with second-half strikes in the 71st and 89th minutes.

Midfielder Michael Bradley, son of U.S. head coach Bob Bradley and a rising start in the German Bundesliga, races past a Trinidad & Tobago defender during the April 2009 qualifier in Nashville.

Costa Rica 3, United States 1

June 3, 2009

Estadio Ricardo Saprissa, San Jose, Costa Rica

Attendance: 19,200

American players are quick to point out that Costa Rica's home field—which features a terrible artificial-turf surface—has to be one of the world's worst, but that's no excuse for the poor performance the U.S. men registered in their June 3, 2009, qualifier. Costa Rica applied intense pressure from the opening whistle and was rewarded with its first goal—a beautiful curling 20-yard strike by Alvaro Saborio—just 79 seconds into the game. When an unmarked Celso Borges added a second score in the 13th minute, the game was all but over.

Pablo Barrantes scored a third time for Costa Rica in the 69th minute, and the United States finally got on the board in injury time. Landon Donovan's penalty conversion was his 10th World Cup qualifying goal—tying him with Brian McBride for the most ever by an American—but it was little consolation in an ugly 3–1 loss. With the victory, Costa Rica jumped to the top of the Hexagonal tables and continued its undefeated streak against the U.S. on its home soil.

The Costa Ricans celebrate Pablo Barrantes' 69th-minute strike that turned their match-up with the United States into a rout.

United States 2, Honduras 1

June 6, 2009

Soldier Field, Chicago, Illinois

Attendance: 55,647

The atmosphere was truly electric for the first U.S. MNT World Cup qualifier ever held in Chicago, and the loud (but well-behaved) crowd was rewarded with an exciting match. The United States, desperate to atone for its recent poor game in Costa Rica, came out aggressively and seemed destined to take control of the contest—until a silly error put the team in an early hole for the third time in five qualifiers. This time the culprit was Clint Dempsey, who botched a back heel in the fifth minute and gifted a breakaway to the Hondurans. Carlos Costly converted and the U.S. was down 1–0.

Unlike its previous game, the U.S. didn't let the error affect them and dug in with greater intensity. After several near misses, the Americans were awarded a penalty in the 43rd minute after an obvious handball. "Mr. Automatic" Landon Donovan converted, and the game was tied at halftime.

The United States didn't let up in the second half, and in the 68th minute a Donovan corner found a leaping Dempsey on the far post; he headed the ball down and toward the middle of the goal mouth, where a diving Carlos Bocanegra put his own head on the ball and tallied what would eventually stand as the winning goal. Yet the final 20 minutes were anything but easy for the Americans, and the large crowd was entertained to the final whistle by Honduras' furious attempts to equalize. When it was over, the U.S. had a satisfying victory and a comfortable hold on second place in CONCACAF qualifying.

Working forward against Honduras' Hendry Thomas, Clint Dempsey looks for a passing lane. Though a miscue by Dempsey helped set up the Hondurans' goal, he atoned for the mistake by helping to set up Carlos Bocanegra for the winner.

Mexico 2, United States 1

August 12, 2009

Estadio Azteca, Mexico City, Mexico

Attendance: 105,000

Much had changed since the easy U.S. victory over Mexico in Columbus six months earlier. Significantly, a coaching change had rejuvenated the Mexicans, who finally looked like a team worthy of a trip to South Africa. The results of two recent international competitions had also altered the competitive landscape. The Americans had gone to South Africa and beaten No. 1–ranked Spain in the Confederations Cup; they followed that up with a strong—though losing—effort in the final against Brazil. Meanwhile, Mexico was the recently crowned CONCACAF Gold Cup champion, a title earned by

drubbing the United States 5–0 in the final. Despite the fact that the U.S. played the tournament with its third-string team, the Mexicans were primed for action.

During the Confederations Cup, the U.S. had found a second young striker to pair with Jozy Altidore—Charlie Davies, and he quickly made his presence felt in Mexico City. In just the ninth minute, a brilliant Landon Donovan through ball fed a perfectly timed Davies run, and his shot from 16 yards gave the U.S. an unlikely 1–0 lead. It was the first time that the United States had ever led at Estadio Azteca and only the fourth U.S. goal in the venue. Unfortunately, the lead held for only 10 minutes when a long Israel Castro shot rocked the underside of the crossbar for the equalizer.

As the game wore on, the huge crowd got uglier and louder, and Mexico patiently ramped up its pressure on the Americans. Inevitably, the noise, high altitude, polluted air, and relentless physical play of the Mexicans started to take their toll on the tiring U.S. squad. Just when a hard-fought draw seemed to be in reach, a well-defended Mexico attack in the box resulted in a quirky bounce and the ball falling to the feet of recent sub Miguel Sabah. He converted, and the 81st-minute goal held for the victory.

Though the loss was frustrating, the United States took consolation in a solid performance in a tough environment. Donovan earned special kudos, especially after it was revealed that he played a full game despite suffering the effects of a case of H1N1 (swine) flu. Yet all that said, the U.S. found itself in an ever-tightening race among four teams for the three automatic CONCACAF World Cup berths.

(above) As the game wore on, it became clear that the United States did not quite have the legs to keep up with a Mexican squad used to playing in the altitude and polluted air of Mexico City. (opposite) Clint Dempsey and Ricardo Clark give chase in the second half. The United States put on a proud performance in front of the hostile crowd, coming just nine minutes short of a draw.

United States 2, El Salvador 1

September 5, 2009

Rio Tinto Stadium, Sandy, Utah

Attendance: 19,066

It was a beautiful Utah night in front of an enthusiastic crowd, but the United States again yielded a first-half goal thanks to sloppy play and found themselves trailing El Salvador. The damage came in the 32nd minute on a Christian Castillo header made possible thanks to a terrible clearance attempt by Jonathan Bornstein.

Fortunately, the gaffe seemed to wake the Americans, and they responded with an offensive fury that led to a 41st-minute equalizer off the head of Clint Dempsey and the game-winner shortly before the half by Jozy Altidore. Beautiful passes from Landon Donovan set up both scores.

The U.S. entered the game without central defender Oguchi Onyewu thanks to a yellow-card suspension and his absence hurt the defense. Carlos Bocanegra moved to the middle and paired with Chad Marshall, playing in his first World Cup qualifier. The duo was solid but the team defensive effort was shaky at times.

In the second half, the U.S. managed to protect its lead but never could completely put away El Salvador. Fortunately, Tim Howard saved a point-blank shot late in the game to preserve the win and put the United States back in first place in the Hexagonal.

Jozy Altidore reacts after his strike just before the half sent the crowd at Rio Tinto Stadium into euphoria. Thanks to timely goalkeeping from Tim Howard, Altidore's goal stood as the game winner.

United States 1, Trinidad & Tobago 0
September 9, 2009

Hasely Crawford Stadium, Port-of-Spain, Trinidad

Attendance: 12,000

With four teams locked in a tight battle for the three automatic CONCACAF spots in South Africa, the U.S. trip to Trinidad seemed to offer the team's best opportunity for a precious road win in this round of qualifying. Plus, Trinidad & Tobago, more or less eliminated from qualifying, fielded a lineup with some new faces, hoping to get some experience for young players.

Unfortunately, the Americans seemingly failed to grasp the opportunity presented to them and sleepwalked through the first half. They went to the locker room at halftime fortunate to be locked in a scoreless tie. T&T had failed to convert two golden opportunities within a span of three minutes. The first shot, by Kenwyne Jones, was saved by Tim Howard. The second, by Cornell Glen, was a beautiful lob over Howard's head that seemed destined for the net but caught the crossbar.

The United States found a little more energy in the second half and was finally rewarded with a lead in the 62nd minute. As usual, Landon Donovan was in the middle of the scoring play, laying off a nice set-up pass to midfielder Ricardo Clark, who rocketed a wicked, curving shot past T&T goalkeeper Clayton Ince. The goal was just the second for Clark in international play, and his timing couldn't have better: his Trinidad-born father, Lance, had made the trip to Port-of-Spain and was in the stands cheering for his son.

The single goal held up until the final whistle. It was anything but a pretty win, but the three points earned kept the U.S. in first place and put it in position to lock up a CONCACAF automatic qualifying spot with one win in its last two games.

Ricardo Clark battles for the ball with Clyde Leon of Trinidad & Tobago at Hasely Crawford Stadium in Trinidad.

United States 3, Honduras 2

October 10, 2009

Estadio Olimpico Metropolitano, San Pedro Sula, Honduras

Attendance: 45,000

The United States booked its ticket to South Africa in dramatic fashion, pulling off an come-from-behind victory on the road against Honduras. The Hondurans went on the attack from the beginning, keeping the U.S. on its heels. Even under pressure, the Americans had the best scoring chance of the first half—when Charlie Davies slammed a rebound off the crossbar—but the U.S. was fortunate to reach halftime in a scoreless draw.

It took Honduras just two minutes to open the second-half scoring, on a Julio Cesar de Leon free kick. The United States pulled level eight minutes later thanks to surprise-starter Conor Casey. The hustling striker beat the keeper to a header from Davies and bounced the ball into the net.

In the 66th minute, Casey struck again. Running on to a beautiful through ball from Landon Donovan, he faked then deftly slipped the ball inside the right post. Donovan made it three straight U.S. goals in the 69th minute thanks to a gorgeous bending free kick. All the U.S. had to do was hold on for 20 minutes...which proved a challenge.

Honduras pressured relentlessly and de Leon delivered a second goal in the 78th minute. In the 87th minute, Stuart Holden's handball in the box looked sure to give Honduras the draw, but Carlos Pavon sent his penalty over the crossbar. The whistle sounded and the United States was bound for South Africa.

Raising his arms in celebration, Stuart Holden runs alongside Landon Donovan, whose 69th minute goal gave the United States the win they needed to qualify for South Africa.

United States 2, Costa Rica 2

October 14, 2009

RFK Stadium, Washington, D.C.

Attendance: 30,000

The last World Cup qualifier took on special meaning for the U.S. squad after Charlie Davies was seriously injured in a car accident, with his teammates declaring that they wanted to win one for the striker. But Costa Rica, needing a victory to qualify for South Africa, seemed more determined to win—especially during a four-minute span in the first half when two Bryan Ruiz goals gave them a 2–0 lead.

Without Davies, the United States struggled offensively. Clint Dempsey was out with a shoulder injury and Jozy Altidore looked rusty. As the second half wound down, Bob Bradley turned to subs Jose Francisco Torres and Robbie Rogers for offensive punch, and the U.S. attack picked up.

The Americans finally broke through in the 72nd minute when Michael Bradley pounced on the rebound of a Landon Donovan shot. Bob Bradley soon used his final sub, Kenny Cooper, but the move backfired when Oguchi Onyewu was injured and carted off the field, leaving the U.S. a man short for the rest of the match.

The shorthanded Americans never let up and earned a draw in dramatic fashion in the fifth minute

of stoppage time. A perfect corner from Rogers found the head of a hard-charging Jonathan Bornstein, who netted the ball from six yards out.

The draw gave the United States first place in CONCACAF, but the achievement was tempered by bad news: Onyewu suffered a torn patellar tendon, leaving him a question mark for South Africa.

Steve Cherundolo and his mates on the back line had a tough task when Oguchi Onyewu went off with an injury against Costa Rica. The Americans responded with stout defending in front of the home crowd to preserve the draw.

South Africa
Historic World Cup Host

Twenty years ago, it would have been unthinkable for South Africa to be hosting the World Cup. In fact, at that time, South Africa did not even have a national soccer team: the country had been expelled from FIFA in 1961 because it refused to field a racially mixed team. The South African constitution actually prohibited creating a team consisting of both white and black members because of its official policy of Apartheid—a legal system mandating racial segregation—that had been instituted in 1948. In 1990 the Apartheid system started to break down, thanks to the efforts of president F.W. De Klerk, who pushed the government toward negotiations with the African National Congress after he freed the organization's leader, Nelson Mandela, from prison.

South Africa's peaceful transition to an ethnically diverse democratic nation is one of the world's great success stories, and it did not go unnoticed by FIFA. In 1991, South Africa was readmitted as a member to soccer's governing body, and in 1992 the country played its first international game in years, defeating Cameroon 1–0. Six years later, South Africa made its first appearance at a World Cup final (France 1998). It repeated this achievement in 2002, but in both tournaments the country failed to advance past the first round.

In 2004 South Africa was the beneficiary of a short-lived plan to rotate the World Cup finals among the five major continents. Because Africa had never before hosted the finals, 2010 was targeted for the continent, and five nations submitted bids. Libya and Tunisia submitted a bid to co-host, while South Africa, Morocco, and Egypt put their names forward as sole-host nations. When FIFA said no to the idea of co-hosts for 2010, Tunisia withdrew. Libya was quickly eliminated when its sole bid failed to meet FIFA's basic requirements. South Africa narrowly defeated Morocco when the FIFA Executive Committee voted on the three remaining participants and earned the right to host the 2010 tournament. It was an amazing reward for a nation aggressively rebuilding itself after years of political turmoil and scorn from the rest of the world.

A centerpiece event for a country that has spent much of the last two decades rebuilding both internally and in the eyes of the world, the 2010 World Cup will showcase South Africa as a proud, diverse country with a strong outlook for the future.

World Cup 2010
Host Cities and Venues

Soccer City: Johannesburg

Capacity: 94,700

Year Built: 1987 (major renovation in 2009)

Games Hosted: Final, quarterfinal, round of 16, group matches (including opening match)

Could there be a more fitting name for a stadium hosting the World Cup final? Located in South Africa's largest city, the venue has been the heart of the national team since it returned to international competition in the early 1990s. It was also where the massive rally was held to honor Nelson Mandela on his release from prison. The design of the unique stadium was inspired by the African cooking pot, the calabash. As originally built, the facility (previously known as FNB Stadium) held 80,000 people. The top tier of the stadium was expanded to enlarge the capacity and then topped with a partial roof. Additional luxury suites and new locker rooms were also part of the upgrade.

Green Point Stadium: Cape Town

Capacity: 70,000

Year Built: New (opened late 2009)

Games Hosted: Semifinal, quarterfinal, round of 16, group matches

This stunning new stadium at the southern tip of Africa was built in one of the most desirable parts of one of the world's most beautiful cities, Cape Town. Located just a short walk from both the ocean and the city's primary transportation hub, Green Point is going to be a outstanding place to watch soccer and will host games throughout almost every phase of the tournament. After the Cup, local clubs Ajax Cape Town and Santos will play at the facility, which will be used for concerts and other major events.

Moses Mabhida Stadium: Durban

Capacity: 70,000

Year Built: New (opened 2009)

Games Hosted: Semifinal, round of 16, group matches

Destined to become one of the world's most memorable sports venues, this new facility's signature element is a massive arch that spans the length of the stadium and tops out at more than 300 feet above the pitch. A viewing platform, served by a cable car, will afford amazing panoramas of both the stadium and the city. Seaside Durban is Africa's busiest port and is blessed with a mild climate that should provide great weather even for a tournament that spills into the South African winter.

Nelson Mandela Bay Stadium: Port Elizabeth

Capacity: 48,000

Year Built: New (opened 2009)

Games Hosted: Third place, quarterfinal, round of 16, group matches

This venue built specifically for the World Cup will be the first soccer-specific stadium in Port Elizabeth, a city of 1 million people located in the Eastern Cape province. Located on the shores of North End Lake, this eye-catching facility boasts a unique partial roof that curves up and around the outside of the structure. The coastal, subtropical city offers a mild winter climate, which should offer pleasant weather for World Cup matches—including the third-place game.

Ellis Park Stadium:
Johannesburg

Capacity: 61,000

Year Built: 1982 (renovated in 2009)

Games Hosted: Quarterfinals, round of 16, group matches

Originally built for rugby in 1982, Ellis Park was given a facelift and expanded by 5,000 seats in 2009. The newly upgraded venue was the site of the exciting Confederations Cup final between the U.S. and Brazil. Located adjacent to the city center of bustling Johannesburg, the facility actually sits on the site of the original Ellis Park Stadium, built in 1928 and demolished to make way for the current facility. The stadium is home to top South African professional club Orlando Pirates.

Free State Stadium:
Mangaung/Bloemfontein

Capacity: 48,000

Year Built: 1952 (renovated in 2008)

Games Hosted: Round of 16, group matches

Mangaung/Bloemfontein is South Africa's judicial capital as well as the capital of Free State Province, and the city's primary soccer facility holds a special place in the hearts of the U.S. Men's National Team: it's where they defeated world No. 1 Spain in the 2009 Confederations Cup. Free State Stadium has been used over the years for both rugby and soccer, though the growing popularity of home club Bloemfontein Celtic has recently pushed soccer to the forefront. In fact, the club's lively fans are recognized as the country's most passionate. The recent renovation added 7,000 seats and transformed Free State Stadium into a world-class facility worthy of Cup matches.

Royal Bafokeng Stadium: Rustenburg

Capacity: 42,000

Year Built: 1999 (renovated in 2010)

Games Hosted: Round of 16, group matches

Loftus Versfeld Stadium: Pretoria (Tshwane)

Capacity: 50,000

Year Built: 1906 (renovated 2008)

Games Hosted: Round of 16, group matches

Rustenberg is a city of about 400,000 people located in the high savannah of the North West Province. It's a major platinum mining center and, in fact, the stadium is named after it owners, the local Bafokeng people who won a legal battle that entitled them to a share of the platinum profits earned from their ancestral lands. The tribe also owns the Platinum Stars soccer team that calls the stadium its home. Though the stadium is relatively new, it received a significant facelift for the World Cup, including a 4,000-seat expansion and a new cantilevered roof over the stands.

Named after Robert Owen Loftus Versfeld, a noted figure in Pretoria rugby who died in the stands during a 1932 game, this stadium is one of the oldest and most historic in South Africa. It has been renovated numerous times, most recently in advance of the 2009 Confederations Cup, when a new roof and lighting system were added. Pretoria is the country's administrative capital and home to more than 2 million people. Winter temperatures are usually mild, but the city sits at an elevation of roughly 4,000 feet above sea level, which might challenge some flatland teams.

Mbombela Stadium: Nelspruit

Capacity: 46,000

Year Built: New

Games Hosted: Group matches

Peter Mokaba Stadium: Polokwane

Capacity: 46,000

Year Built: New

Games Hosted: Group matches

Mbombela means "many people together in a small space" in the local siSwati language, an apt description for this beautiful new soccer stadium. This facility, built specifically for the World Cup, is yet another South African showpiece, featuring a segmented flat roof covering most of the stands. Nelspruit (population 220,000) is the capital of Mpumalanga Province and the smallest city hosting World Cup matches. Located in the northeast part of the country and close to world-famous game reserves, the subtropical climate will provide comfortable temperatures, even for the winter matches.

Polokwane has a population of roughly half a million and is located in the grasslands of he Limpopo Province in the northeast corner of the country. This beautiful, brand-new stadium was built adjacent to the site of an older facility with the same moniker—a tribute to a native son who played a key role in the fight against Apartheid. Built at a cost of $145 million, the stadium will host four first-round matches, one each from Groups A, B, C, and F.

Soccer permeates all layers of the cosmopolitan South African society.

Confederations Cup
U.S. Shines in World Cup Warm-up

The FIFA Confederations Cup has evolved into a World Cup dress rehearsal held one year in advance of the tournament. The 2009 competition gave South Africans an opportunity to prove that they were ready for the main event. It also promised some great soccer, with eight top teams competing—the host country, 2006 champion, Italy, and the winners of the most recent tournaments from the six global confederations: Spain (Europe), Brazil (South America), Iraq (Asia), New Zealand (Oceania), Egypt (Africa), and the United States (CONCACAF).

Spain and Brazil entered the tournament ranked 1 and 2, respectively. Both powerhouses went undefeated during the group stage (teams were split into two four-team groups) and appeared on track to meet in the finals. Meanwhile, the U.S. stumbled badly, losing 3–1 to Italy and 3–0 to Brazil, and looked en route to a quick exit. Going into their final group stage match against Egypt, the Americans needed a miracle to advance to the knockout round...and that's what they got.

In fact, the U.S. benefited from two miracles. The first was a complete rebirth on the pitch against Egypt that resulted in a 3–0 rout of the African champions. Meanwhile, Italy disintegrated against Brazil, also losing 3–0. When the final whistles sounded on both games, the Americans advanced to the next round because they had scored one more goal than the Italians.

Waiting for the U.S. in the semifinals was European-champion Spain. Yet the Americans rose to the challenge, playing possibly the best game in U.S. team history in winning 2–0. Jozy Altidore opened the scoring in the 27th minute and Clint Dempsey sealed the deal with another strike in the 74th minute.

Advancing to the finals, the U.S. faced a rematch with Brazil. Looking like a very different team, the American attacked the Brazilians from the opening whistle. Clint Dempsey drew first blood just 10 minutes into the match. Landon Donovan added a second goal 17 minutes later, and the U.S. went into halftime with a 2–0 advantage.

Brazil scored its first goal just a minute into the second half and eventually overwhelmed the U.S. with its offensive firepower. The Americans played well but not well enough to beat the world's best team. They fell 3–2.

Regardless of the outcome in the final, the U.S. team left the Confederations Cup with their heads held high and possessing the confidence that they could compete with—and defeat—the world's best squads.

USA defender Jay DeMerit and the rest of the back line battled valiantly—but ultimately, unsuccessfully—to hold the lead in the second half of the 2009 Confederations Cup final against Brazil.

World Cup 2010
The Qualifiers

Though it probably escaped the attention of many Americans, the December 4, 2009, draw to determine the team groupings for the 2010 FIFA World Cup was one of the most highly anticipated sports-related events on the planet. The irony is that, like the NFL Draft every spring, the event is popular with fans even though no contest of any kind actually takes place—basically, names are selected and placed on a board. And unlike the NFL Draft, the World Cup draw is based largely on luck. Fans analyze and agonize over the outcome, but apart from seeding and geographical constraints, all the teams are at the mercy of a random draw.

Yet the whole drama involved in the draw makes for good theater, and FIFA and South Africa played up the 90-minute event (which included just a few actual minutes of team drawing) to full affect. The more than 200 million people watching the live television broadcast (with countless more tracking the event on the Internet) were treated to a full-blown extravaganza from Cape Town, including music and celebrities of all types—retired soccer greats, Nobel Prize winners, notable politicians, and more. South African–born Academy

Award–winner Charlize Theron was the guest presenter; David Beckham joined her onstage for added star power.

In the end, South Africa delivered one of the more equitable and interesting draws seen in recent years. It was difficult to immediately anoint a "group of death" overloaded with three or four high-ranking teams. Probably the closest to deserving this moniker was Group G, with tournament favorite Brazil, European power Portugal, and quality African squad Ivory Coast all predraw picks to advance to the Round of 16. Mexico was probably the happiest of the CONCACAF teams after getting slotted with host South Africa rather than one of the top seven seeds. Even so, France and Uruguay make Group A very competitive.

As for the U.S., getting drawn into Group C with England, Algeria, and Slovenia seemed to be a fantastic result—especially compared to 2006's "group of death" draw with Italy, the Czech Republic, and Ghana. During the run-up to the draw, American soccer commentators seemed resigned to the U.S. getting stuck in another tough group, as if there was some conspiracy against the Americans and a way for FIFA to control its random

draw. But once the results were posted, U.S. fans breathed a big sigh of relief.

While it's never a good idea for a team to get too optimistic before a World Cup—especially the U.S., which has played inconsistently and has a host of injury concerns—Group C looks like one that the Americans can advance from. One positive aspect of this group is that the games won't require a huge amount travel around South Africa and will be contested in venues in which the U.S. played during last year's Confederations Cup.

The biggest challenge for the U.S. will be opening the tournament against England on June 12.

As was obvious at the Confederations Cup, the U.S. team can require a game or two to get on track. Yet, as far as the seeded teams go, England is a nice matchup for the Americans. Several members of the U.S MNT are familiar with England's players and style of play because they compete in the EPL or Championship League. Slovenia and Algeria are both quality sides and worthy Cup qualifiers, but they are teams against which the U.S. should be favored to win. Beating both should be enough to ensure advancement to the knockout stage no matter the result against England.

The star-studded World Cup draw—co-hosted by South African actress Charlize Theron—elicited a sigh of relief from U.S. fans. Group C, with England, Algeria, and Slovenia, seemed a good spot for the Americans.

Qualifying-Team Capsules

Algeria

Population (2009): 34.9 million	
Capital: Algiers	

Nickname: Les Fennecs (The Desert Foxes)

Qualifying Region: Africa/CAF

FIFA World Cups Hosted: None

Previous World Cup Appearances (2): 1982, 1986

Top Finish: Round 1, 1982 and 1986

Most-Capped Player (107): Mahieddine Meftah, 1989–2006

Most Goals (35): Abdelhafid Tasfaout, 1990–2002

Algeria was one of the last teams booked for the 2010 World Cup finals, having negotiated a difficult road through qualifying. They ended Africa's third round tied dead square in their group with Egypt, forcing a playoff game in neutral Sudan between the fierce rivals. The Desert Foxes advanced with a stunning 1–0 victory in the playoff. The team seems to be peaking at the right time, having recently cracked FIFA's top 30 for the first time, and Algerians are optimistic of surpassing the country's 1980s glory years when the team qualified for two World Cups—only to exit in the first round in each competition. Instability at the top is the team's biggest problem: coach Rabah Saadane is in the midst of his fifth different stint leading the team. The player pool is more stable and features a mixture of talent from the top Algerian clubs and various European teams. Midfielder Yazid Mouri, who plays for French club FC Lorient and is the most-capped active Algerian player, captains the team. Defender Anthar Yahia (Bochum, Germany) provides surprising offensive punch; his thrilling long-distance volley proved the game-winner over Egypt.

Argentina

Population (2009): 40.5 million	
Capital: Buenos Aires	

Nickname: Albicelestes (White and Sky Blue)

Qualifying Region: South America/CONMEBOL

FIFA World Cups Hosted (1): 1978

Previous World Cup Appearances (14): 1930, 1934, 1958, 1962, 1966, 1974, 1978, 1982, 1986, 1990, 1994, 1998, 2002, 2006

Championships (2): 1978, 1986

Most-Capped Player (136): Javier Zanetti, 1994–

Most Goals (56): Gabriel Batistuta, 1991–2002

Argentina boasts one of the planet's most impressive soccer legacies—14 World Cup appearances, two championships, and several of the game's all-time greats—yet the men in blue and white looked anything but impressive during the qualifying rounds. After bowing out in the quarterfinals of World Cup 2006, Alfio Basile took over the team and led them to the FIFA No. 1 ranking in 2007. But after losing to Brazil in that year's Copa America finals, Argentina slid into a doldrums that continued into CONMEBOL qualifying. When Basile resigned in late 2008, Diego Maradona, the country's greatest soccer hero, was handed the reins. His tenure has been a controversial roller-coaster ride, but the team recovered adequately from a three-game losing streak to sneak into the final South American qualifying spot. Despite the chaos at the helm, Argentina is blessed with its usual overload of talent, including striker Lionel Messi (Barcelona), arguably the world's best player. Providing support to its youthful scoring threats are an experienced midfield and back line, led by captain Javier Mascherano (Liverpool) and rock-solid defenseman Gabriel Heinze (Marseilles). Despite their recent mixed form, the Argentines will arrive in South Africa as one of the outside favorites to win it all and should have an easy time advancing from Group B to the Round of 16.

Australia

Population (2009): 21.8 million	
Capital: Canberra	

Nickname: Socceroos

Qualifying Region: Asia/AFC

FIFA World Cups Hosted: None

Previous World Cup Appearances (2): 1974, 2006

Top Finish: Round of 16, 2006

Most-Capped Player (87): Alex Tobin, 1988–1998

Most Goals (29): Damian Mori, 1992–2002

This was Australia's first campaign since gaining membership into the Asian Football Confederation, and the team earned automatic qualification by handily winning Asia

World Cup 2010
First-Round Groups

Group A	Group E
South Africa	Netherlands
Mexico	Denmark
Uruguay	Japan
France	Cameroon

Group B	Group F
Argentina	Italy
Nigeria	Paraguay
South Korea	New Zealand
Greece	Slovakia

Group C	Group G
England	Brazil
USA	North Korea
Algeria	Ivory Coast
Slovenia	Portugal

Group D	Group H
Germany	Spain
Australia	Switzerland
Serbia	Honduras
Ghana	Chile

U.S. First-Round
Game Schedule

Saturday, June, 12—Rustenburg

U.S. vs. England

Friday, June 18—Johannesburg/Ellis Park

U.S. vs. Slovenia

Wednesday, June 23—Tshwane/Pretoria

U.S. vs. Algeria

Group A, amassing 20 points with six wins and two draws in eight games. Brett Emerton (midfield, Blackburn/EPL) led the way with four goals; Harry Kewell (midfield, Galatasaray/Turkey) chipped in three during qualifying. The country has high expectations for the 2010 Cup, especially in light of its outstanding showing in Germany in 2006. Australia was coached for that tournament by Dutchman Guus Hiddink, now the coach of the Russian national team and in 2009 the successful interim leader for EPL squad Chelsea. Graham Arnold and Rob Baan served as interim coaches after Hiddink's departure, but in 2007 Australia settled on another Dutchman, Pim Verbeek, who was most recently the coach of South Korea. Germany is the clear favorite in Group D, but Australia is optimistic that it can outmaneuver Serbia and Ghana for second place and a berth in the knockout stage.

Brazil

Population (2009): 191 million

Capital: Sao Paolo

Nickname: A Selecao

Qualifying Region: South America/CONMEBOL

FIFA World Cups Hosted (1): 1950 (also awarded 2014 Cup)

Previous World Cup Appearances (19): 1930, 1934, 1938, 1942, 1950, 1954, 1958, 1962, 1966, 1970, 1974, 1978, 1982, 1986, 1990, 1994, 1998, 2002, 2006

Championships (5): 1958, 1962, 1970, 1994, 2002

Most-Capped Player (142): Cafu, 1990–2006

Most Goals (77): Pele, 1957–1971

With its victory in the June 2009 Confederations Cup tournament, Brazil earned the FIFA No. 1 ranking and established itself as the early favorite to win a record sixth World Cup title in 2010. The Green-Blue-and-Yellow's 1–0 quarterfinal loss in Germany at the hands of France left most Brazilians feeling like the 2006 tournament was a huge failure, thus the focus on South Africa. New coach Dunga, a star player with the 1994 championship team, has shaken up the roster, filling it out with lesser-known players who have infused the side with much-needed energy. Sevilla's Luis Fabiano, for example, led the team in scoring during the qualifying round. Nonetheless, the team's fortunes continue to ride on the shoulders of its biggest stars—especially Kaka (Real Madrid), who was named outstanding player of the Confederations Cup. In the qualifying round, Brazil led the way in the always-competitive South American region, losing just once in 18 games. That outstanding performance is bad news for the rest of the world. While Group G has two other teams (Portugal and Ivory Coast) with the credentials to advance, Brazil should have no problem wrapping up the top spot and a ticket to Stage 2.

Brazil's Kaka was named the most outstanding player at the Confederations Cup in 2009 and he is no stranger to the international stage as he appears in his third World Cup this summer. He has won Europe's Ballon d'Or and was named FIFA's World Player of the Year in 2007.

Cameroon

Population (2009): 19.5 million

Capital: Yaounde

Nickname: Indomitable Lions

Qualifying Region: Africa/CAF

FIFA World Cups Hosted: None

Previous World Cup Appearances (5): 1982, 1990, 1994, 1998, 2002

Top Finish: Quarterfinals, 1990

Most-Capped Player (129): Rigobert Song, 1993–

Most Goals (41): Samuel Eto'o, 1996–

Chile

Population (2009): 16.9 million

Capital: Santiago

Nickname: La Roja (The Red)

Qualifying Region: South America/CONMEBOL

FIFA World Cups Hosted (1): 1962

Previous World Cup Appearances (7): 1930, 1950, 1962, 1966, 1974, 1982, 1998

Top Finish: Third Place, 1962

Most-Capped Player (84): Leonel Sanchez, 1955–1968

Most Goals (37): Marcelo Salas, 1994–2007

Among African nations, Cameroon boasts the most World Cup appearances as well as the best finish in the tournament—they reached the quarterfinals in 1990. Yet since that high-water mark two decades ago, the Indomitable Lions have failed to progress out of the first round in three subsequent Cup appearances. In 2010, Cameroon won a relatively weak Africa Group A, but not before a couple of poor performances prompted a coaching change, with Paul Le Guen replacing Otto Pfister. Le Guen quickly stirred things up with a controversial move—handing the captain's armband to the team's marquee player and all-time leading scorer, striker Samuel Eto'o (Inter Milan). Eto'o replaced veteran defender and all-time cap leader Rigobert Song (Trabzonspor, Turkey) as captain. The switch was not without its critics, but the move seemed to energize both players and the entire squad, which is riding a wave of confidence. Not only will Cameroon enter the first World Cup contested in Africa as the continent's highest-ranked squad, they should be a favorite to slip past Denmark and Japan in Group E and make a run at being the first African semifinalist.

Chile was the third country to secure a spot in South Africa out of the always-competitive South American region, but predicting La Roja as a qualifier as recently as 2007 might have been greeted with laughs. The team was in turmoil after the Copa America tournament. Six players were given long-term disciplinary suspensions, and coach Nelson Acosta was forced to resign. Enter former Argentina head man Marcelo Bielsa, who was given the tough task of turning around the team's fortunes in time for Cup qualifying—and thus far has succeeded beyond most Chileans' expectations. His secret ingredient for success? Youth—all of the current regulars will be younger than 30 when the Cup kicks off. The team is driven by its talented striker tandem of 28-year-old Humberto Suazo (Monterrey, Mexico), who is the leading scorer, and Alexis Sanchez (Udinese, Italy), who is already scaring defenders at the age of 20. Captain and seasoned international veteran (39 caps) goalkeeper Claudio Bravo (Real Sociedad, Spain) is all of 26 years old. Despite its youth, this team is confident for a deep run in the

Striker Samuel Eto'o, a star with Italian squad Inter Milan, was named Cameroon's captain during World Cup qualifying. The decision was controversial but seemed to invigorate the team.

tournament and should be a favorite to advance out of Group H along with Spain. And no matter what the result in South Africa, it may be safe to already count Chile among the favorites for World Cup 2014 in Brazil.

Denmark

Population (2009): 5.5 million

Capital: Copenhagen

Nickname: Danish Dynamite

Qualifying Region: Europe/UEFA

FIFA World Cups Hosted: None

World Cup Appearances (3): 1986, 1998, 2002

Top Finish: Quarterfinals, 1998

Most-Capped Player (129): Peter Schmeichel, 1987–2001

Most Goals (52): Poul "Tist" Nielsen, 1910–1925

Soccer fans in Denmark had little reason to be optimistic as their country began qualifying for the 2010 World Cup. The Danish talent pool looked as lean as had been seen since before the 1980s, when Denmark elevated itself into the top level of European soccer. The UEFA Group One draw didn't do the team any favors; Portugal, Sweden, and Hungary all figured to have stronger squads. Yet the Danish fans had forgotten their secret weapon: Morten Olsen, current team coach and captain of Denmark's first (1986) World Cup squad. Olsen was no less than brilliant in managing a squad lacking star power and further sapped by injuries throughout qualifying. He played 35 players during the first six qualifying matches, emphasizing

not individual performance but tenacious, organized team play. The concept fits the low-key, collectivist Danes, and as a group they responded by clinching Group One with a game to play. Team leaders including Jon Dahl Tomasson (Feyenoord, Netherlands), Dennis Rommedahl (Ajax, Netherlands), and Christian Paulsen (Juventus) aren't exactly household names in Europe, but they are experienced, solid performers who give Denmark hope that they can deliver the country's best World Cup finish in the 2010 tournament.

England

Population (2009): 51.2 million

Capital: London

Nickname: The Three Lions

Qualifying Region: Europe/UEFA

FIFA World Cups Hosted (1): 1966

Previous World Cup Appearances (12): 1950, 1954, 1958, 1962, 1966, 1970, 1982, 1986, 1990, 1998, 2002, 2006

Championships (1): 1966

Most-Capped Player (125): Peter Shilton 1970–1990

Most Goals (49): Bobby Charlton, 1958–1970

England ran amok in UEFA Group Six, clinching first place with its eighth win in eight games, a 5–1 drubbing of second-place Croatia. Looking forward to 2010 and South Africa, the team finds itself in a similar position to 2006. England went to Germany with championship dreams but bowed out in the quarterfinals. Popular

England's World Cup hopes rest squarely on the shoulders of fiery Manchester United striker Wayne Rooney, who has matured and mellowed in recent years while maintaining his high level of play.

manager Sven-Goran Eriksson was sacked and replaced by Steve McClaren, who had a disastrous six-month run at the top. England then turned to Italian Fabio Capello, who has righted the ship and started the English thinking about winning the Cup again. Capello announced that the trip to South Africa was not a holiday and that contact with family and girlfriends would be limited, hopefully heading off the media circus that usually surrounds the team. On the pitch, the squad has multiple weapons. Yes, midfielder and set-piece specialist David Beckham (L.A. Galaxy/AC Milan) is likely to be back on the squad, but at 34 his best play is behind him. Instead, England will count on hard-nosed captain/defender John Terry (Chelsea), offensive-minded midfielders Steven Gerrard (Liverpool) and Frank Lampard (Chelsea), and pugnacious striker Wayne Rooney (Manchester United) to carry them deep into the tournament.

France

Population (2009): 65.1 million	
Capital: Paris	

Nickname: Les Bleus (The Blues)

Qualifying Region: Europe/UEFA

FIFA World Cups Hosted (2): 1938, 1998

Previous World Cup Appearances (12): 1930, 1934, 1938, 1954, 1958, 1966, 1978, 1982, 1986, 1998, 2002, 2006

Championships (1): 1998

Most-Capped Player (142): Lillian Thuram, 1994–2008

Most Goals (51): Thierry Henry, 1997–

France consistently ranks among the world's top soccer squads, but many would argue that they don't deserve their spot in South Africa—notably members of Ireland's national team. Despite their talented lineup, France struggled in qualifying, finished second in UEFA Group Seven, and faced a playoff with the Irish for a spot in the finals. France took the first leg 1–0 in Dublin but was down a goal—thus tied on aggregate—in extra time in Paris when an obviously offside Thierry Henry (Barcelona) purposely handled a pass then fed defender William Gallas (Arsenal) for the winning goal. The officials missed the infractions, and France was in the World Cup. A chagrined Henry admitted his transgression and suggested a replay, but FIFA wasn't interested. In addition to the controversy, France will enter the tournament dogged by questions attributable to its uneven play of late. Lack of talent is not a problem for France. In addition to Henry and Gallas, striker Nicolas Anelka (Chelsea), midfielder Franck Ribery (Bayern Munich) and defender Patrice Evra (Manchester United) are just some of the players that comprise—on paper at least—one of the world's top soccer teams. Whether France will flame out or contend for the championship will be one of the more interesting storylines of World Cup 2010. A fortunate draw into Group A with South Africa, Mexico, and Uruguay make them a favorite to advance to the Round of 16, but how France performs after that is anyone's guess.

Thierry Henry created a scandal with his offside/handball/goal assist that sent the Irish to defeat in a qualifying playoff, but France remains an elite team, having posted a championship and runner-up showing in two of the last three World Cups.

Germany

Population (2009): 82 million

Capital: Berlin

Nickname: Die Mannschaft (The Team)

Qualifying Region: Europe/UEFA

FIFA World Cups Hosted (2): 1974, 2006

Previous World Cup Appearances (16): 1934, 1938, 1954, 1958, 1962, 1966, 1970, 1974, 1978, 1982, 1986, 1990, 1994, 1998, 2002, 2006

Championships (3): 1954, 1974, 1990

Most-Capped Player (150): Lothar Matthaus, 1980–2000

Most Goals (68): Gerd Muller, 1966–1974

Germany ranks alongside Brazil and Italy in terms of all-time excellence in the World Cup. The country's record is amazing: 16 appearances, three championships, and four second-place finishes. Only once has Germany failed to advance out of the first round (1938), and only twice has the team failed to reach the round of 16 (1978 being the only other time). In 2006 Germany hosted the finals, but its team was in the midst of a downward cycle and lightly regarded...only to emerge as one of the Cup's pleasant surprises with a solid third-place finish. Since 2006 Joachim Low moved from assistant to head coach after Jurgen Klinsmann decided not to renew his contract, and Germany finished as runner-up to Spain in the Euro 2008 tournament. World Cup qualifying did not go as smoothly as expected, and Germany did not clinch the championship of relatively weak Group Four until

the next-to-last game. There was some discord as Low introduced new players into the lineup, including Bayer Leverkusen goalkeeper Rene Adler, but veterans will ultimately key Germany's success. Michael Ballack (Chelsea) and Bastian Schweinsteiger (Bayern Munich) anchor the midfield, and the front line is manned by the dangerous tandem of Miroslav Klose (Bayern Munich) and Lukas Podolski (Cologne). Not surprisingly, the experienced foursome provided the bulk of Germany's goals during qualifying. It's a group of players talented enough to net the country a fourth World Cup title.

Ghana

Population (2009): 23.8 million

Capital: Accra

Nickname: The Black Stars

Qualifying Region: Africa/CAF

FIFA World Cups Hosted: None

Previous World Cup Appearances (1): 2006

Top Finish: Round 2, 2006

Most-Capped Player (73): Abedi Pele, 1982–1998

Most Goals (33): Abedi Pele

Ghana is a latecomer to the World Cup, having qualified only for the 2006 tournament in Germany, but its youth teams have enjoyed considerable success in international tournaments. Ghana has twice won the Under-17 World Cup, has twice been runner-up in the Under-20 World Cup, and won the bronze medal in the 1992 Olympics. They've also won

Polish-born Lukas Podolski's goals are the stuff of legend among German fans. His pairing with fellow striker Miroslav Klose—who was also born in Poland—makes Germany a potent offensive threat at the World Cup.

more African Nations Cups than any other team, four in all. Ghana was the first African team (except for the automatic-qualifying hosts) to qualify for the tournament, clinching first place in Group D after winning its first four games. Ghana is coached by Serbian Milovan Rajevac and features a roster filled with regulars from a variety of top-level European clubs. The heart of the team is its talented midfield. Ghana's biggest international star is Chelsea's Michael Essien, not a noted goal scorer but a rock of a holding midfielder. Providing offensive punch from the middle are Inter Milan's Sulley Muntari and team captain Stephen Appiah. The latter has been struggling to recover from a knee injury, but if he regains his 2006 form, look for the Black Stars to make some noise in South Africa. Group D will be a challenge for Ghana (with Germany the clear favorite), but they should have a realistic chance to better Australia and Serbia and advance to Stage 2.

Greece

Population (2009): 11.3 million	
Capital: Athens	

Nickname: The Pirate Ship

Qualifying Region: Europe/UEFA

FIFA World Cups Hosted: None

Previous World Cup Appearances (1): 1994

Top Finish: Round 1, 1994

Most-Capped Player (120): Theodoros Zagorakis, 1994–2007

Most Goals (29): Nikos Anastopoulos, 1977–1988

Greece has made one brief appearance in just a single World Cup, but they shouldn't be overlooked. Europe's soccer powers discovered this fact the hard way when the Greeks stunned the favorites and captured the Euro 2004 crown. Though Greece failed to qualify for the 2006 Cup, they rebounded nicely this time around, finishing second to Switzerland in UEFA Group Two and earning a berth in South Africa with a playoff win over favored Ukraine. The key to Greece's success is their coach, 71-year-old German legend Otto Rehhegel. Called stubborn and criticized for playing "boring" defensive-minded soccer, Rehhegel is quick to answer his critics. "We will play exciting football when we have Messi, Kaka, Iniesta, and Xavi on the team," he once declared, suggesting that his tactics were perfect for the talent on his Greek team. Rehhegel favors veterans who know his system—such as captain/midfielder Giorgos Karagounis (Panathinaikos)—but was not afraid to inject fresh blood into the lineup during qualifying. Defenders Sokratis Papastathopoulos (Genoa) and Vangelis Moras (Bologna) together have earned fewer than 20 caps but were outstanding in the Ukraine playoff matches. There is more to Greece than defense—Theofanis Gekas (Bayer Leverkusen) led all scorers in European qualifying with 10 goals—which is why opponents will find them a tough matchup in South Africa. The Greeks should have a strong shot at a top-two finish (along with favorite Argentina) in Group B and advancement to the Round of 16.

The Euro 2004 champions, Greece may not boast many flashy offensive weapons, but their tough defensive style earns them international admiration—and enough wins to gain the nation's second World Cup bid.

Honduras

Population: 7.8 million

Capital: Tegucigalpa

Nickname: Los Catrachos

Qualifying Region: CONCACAF

FIFA World Cups Hosted: None

Previous FIFA World Cup Appearances (1): 1982

Top Finish: Round 1, 1982

Most-Capped Player (129): Arnado Guevara, 1994–

Most Goals (56): Carlos Pavon, 1993–

Honduras qualified for the 2010 World Cup amidst a backdrop of political turmoil that included a June 2009 military coup and an ongoing dispute over the country's leadership. Nonetheless, the soccer team stayed focused and finished third in the CONCACAF region behind the U.S. and Mexico, earning an automatic bid. The team traveling to South Africa is probably the most talented in the small country's history and will likely prove a major challenge for Spain, Switzerland, and Chile in the group stage. Two veterans—the most-capped Hondurans of all time—lead the team. Midfielder and team captain Arnado Guevara (Toronto FC) has been an MLS mainstay since 2003. Striker Carlos Pavon has been somewhat of an underachieving vagabond in his club career, but he's a dangerous scoring threat when playing for his home country. His goal in the last qualifying game against El Salvador won the game and clinched the Cup bid. The team's best-known players are striker David Suazo (Inter Milan) and midfielder Wilson Palacios. Suazo missed several months after a March 2009 knee injury, but

he was back in action last fall. Palacios persevered despite living through the horror of his younger brother's kidnapping and murder. In addition to his excellence on the international stage, he is a key player for Tottenham Hotspur of the EPL.

Italy

Population (2009): 60.1 million

Capital: Rome

Nickname: Azzurri (Blues)

Qualifying Region: Europe/UEFA

FIFA World Cups Hosted (2): 1934, 1990

Previous World Cup Appearances (16): 1934, 1938, 1950, 1954, 1962, 1966, 1970, 1974, 1978, 1982, 1986, 1990, 1994, 1998, 2002, 2006

Championships (4): 1934, 1938, 1982, 2006

Most-Capped Player (129): Fabio Cannavaro, 1997–

Most Goals (35): Luigi Riva, 1965–1974

Italy captured the first two World Cups it entered but fell into a long soccer doldrums (thanks in large part to WWII) from which the country did not emerge until its runner-up finish in 1970. Over the last 40 years the Azzurri have been one of the world's dominant teams, qualifying for every Cup and failing to advance out of the first round only once. One of the reason's for the country's success is that most of its players stay at home to play club ball—and why not? Serie A is one of the world's top leagues. Currently, only two of the team's regulars play outside of Italy (both strikers): veteran Luca Toni (Bayern Munich) and exciting newcomer Giuseppe Rossi (Villareal), who—remarkably—was born and raised in New Jersey but decided to play

Arguably the best goalkeeper in the world, Gianluigi Buffon is a key reason why it is so difficult to score on the Italians.

for his parents' home country. Toni and Rossi are goal scorers, but the name of the game for Italy is hard-nosed defense. It all starts in front of the net with Gianluigi Buffon (Juventus), arguably the world's top goalkeeper. The back line is packed with experienced, quality defenders, most notably Fabiano Cannavaro (Juventus). The 36-year-old was FIFA World Player of the Year in 2006, making him the oldest player and only defender to ever win the award. The midfield boasts nearly as much international experience. Andrea Pirlo (AC Milan) and Daniele De Rossi (Roma) provide the offensive punch, but the muscle comes from hard-tacking Gennaro Gattuso (AC Milan). This team has all the tools to repeat as champions, but time is running out on many of these players, several of whom might be playing in their last World Cup.

Ivory Coast was identified as a dark horse with the potential to go far—until it drew the dreaded "group of death" that included Argentina and the Netherlands and went out in the first round. Optimism remains high for 2010, though Ghana again finds itself with a tough draw, landing in Group G along with Brazil, Portugal, and North Korea. Nonetheless, Ghana is hoping to better its 2006 performance during the first World Cup finals held in Africa. Keying the Elephants will be one of the world's elite strikers, team captain Didier Drogba. The Chelsea star is the Ivory Coast's all-time scoring leader, and when he's on his game he's nearly unstoppable. Yet, this is far from a one-man team. The midfield is keyed by two La Liga stars, Didier Zokora (Sevilla) and Yaya Toure (Barcelona), and the defense is anchored by a pair of EPL standouts, Emmanuel Eboue (Arsenal) and Kolo Toure (Manchester City).

Ivory Coast

Population (2009): 21.1 million	
Capital: Yamoussoukro	

Nickname: The Elephants

Qualifying Region: Africa/CAF

FIFA World Cups Hosted: None

Previous World Cup Appearances (1): 2006

Top Finish: Round 1, 2006

Most-Capped Player (94): Didier Zokora, 2000–

Most Goals (41): Didier Drogba, 2002–

Japan

Population (2009): 127.6 million	
Capital: Tokyo	

Nickname: Blue Samurai

Qualifying Region: Asia/AFC

FIFA World Cups Hosted (1): 2002 (co-hosted with South Korea)

Previous World Cup Appearances (3): 1998, 2002, 2006

Top Finish: Round of 16, 2002

Most-Capped Player (123): Masami Ihara, 1988–1999

Most Goals (75): Kunishige Kamamoto, 1964–1977

These are heady times for soccer fans in the Ivory Coast. Though a relatively small country, the nation has in recent years exported an impressive collection of talent to the top European leagues, which in turn has allowed it to field an exceptional national team. In Germany 2006, the

Japan earned an automatic bid to South Africa by finishing second in Asia's Group A, accumulating 15 points in eight qualifying matches. Soccer has been on the rise in Japan over the last two decades, in large because of the

Chelsea star Didier Drogba netted six goals in five qualification games for the Ivory Coast and helped lead the Elephants to the quarterfinals of the African Cup of Nations.

successful 1993 launch of the professional J. League. In recent years, Japan has won three Asian Cups and been runner-up in the Confederations Cup (2001) and Under-20 World Cup. This will mark the country's fourth straight appearance in the senior world tournament, and they've become one of the teams that nobody relishes playing because of their aggressive, high-quality play. The individual players are less well known than other international squads because a majority of the team plays for clubs in the J. League, which doesn't enjoy the media attention of the European leagues. The current best-known Japanese player (as well as Japan's active career scoring leader with 23 goals) is Shunsake Nakamura. The winger has played in Italy (Reggina) and Scotland (Celtic) and is now with Espanyol of Spain's La Liga. Group E—also featuring the Netherlands, Denmark, and Cameroon—looks wide open, giving the Japanese optimism for a Round of 16 appearance.

Mexico

Population: 111 million	
Capital: Mexico City	

Nickname: El Tri (The Tricolor)

FIFA World Cups Hosted (2): 1970, 1986

Previous World Cup Appearances (13): 1930, 1950, 1954, 1958, 1962, 1966, 1970, 1978, 1986, 1994, 1998, 2002, 2006

Top Finish: Quarterfinals, 1970 and 1986

Most-Capped Player (178): Claudio Suarez, 1992–2006

Most Goals (46): Jared Borgetti, 1997–

In the spring of 2009, Mexico was a team in disarray. After losing two of its first three Hexagonal qualifying matches, Mexico fired coach Sven-Goran Eriksson and replaced the taciturn Swede with fiery former coach Javier Aguirre. The team lost a third time, then righted the ship over the summer, winning a reinvigorating championship in the CONCACAF Gold Cup. Mexico won five and drew once in its remaining qualifying games to lock up second place in the region and a trip to South Africa. Rehiring Aguirre may have been the key move, but two very different players contributed greatly to the team's return to form. The ageless Cuauhtemoc Blanco (Veracruz) was recalled from international retirement in June 2009, and he provided three goals and a priceless steadying influence. And supremely gifted youngster Giovani Dos Santos (who will be 21 during the Cup finals) finally fulfilled the promise he had been flashing since making his Mexico debut in 2008. Two marquee-quality talents man the Mexican back line. Barcelona's Rafael Marquez is one of the world's top defenders; in 2007 he was among the nominees for FIFA World Player of the Year. Carlos Salcido (PSV Eindhoven) is also an excellent defender, but he also contributed the goal that earned Mexico a draw with Trinidad & Tobago. Along with a talented roster, Mexico will travel to South Africa with a burning desire to re-establish its reputation as CONCACAF's top team—they should be a serious threat to advance out of Group A to the Round of 16 and beyond.

Veteran midfielder Cuauhtemoc Blanco was coaxed out of international retirement in June 2009, and his play rejuvenated Mexico and propelled them to a second-place finish in the CONCACAF region.

Netherlands

Population (2009): 16.5 million

Capital: Amsterdam

Nickname: Orange

Qualifying Region: Europe/UEFA

FIFA World Cups Hosted: None

Previous World Cup Appearances (8): 1934, 1938, 1974, 1978, 1990, 1994, 1998, 2006

Top Finish: Runners-Up, 1974 and 1978

Most-Capped Player (130): Edwin van der Sar, 1995–2008

Most Goals (40): Patrick Kluivert, 1994–2004

The Dutch—the purveyors of "Total Football"—may be more responsible for the exciting state of modern soccer than any other country, but they've never enjoyed a World Cup championship. Twice in the 1970s, brilliant coach Rinus Michels and his star player Johann Cruyff led the Orange to the Cup final, only to fall short of victory. A new generation of the stars returned the Netherlands to glory in the 1990s, but again a championship eluded the team. Despite these earlier disappointments, Dutch optimism is again ascendant, especially with the team's dominance of European Group Nine—they were the first team from Europe to earn an automatic bid to South Africa. A coaching change—Bert van Marwijk replacing Marco van Basten—after a disappointing finish in Euro 2008 has keyed the team's recent resurgence. The team is packed with elite offensive talent. Midfielder Rafael van der Vaart (Real Madrid), striker Robin van Persie (Arsenal), midfielder Wesley Sneijder (Inter Milan), and winger Arjen Robben (Bayern Munich)

are all threats to put the ball in the back of the net—though van Persie suffered an ankle injury in November that makes him a question mark for the Cup. Nonetheless, the Netherlands is the clear favorite in Group E, and many Dutch rightfully feel that 2010 may finally be their year to win it all.

New Zealand

Population (2009): 4.3 million

Capital: Wellington

Nickname: All Whites

Qualifying Region: Oceania

FIFA World Cups Hosted: None

Previous World Cup Appearances (1): 1982

Top Finish: Round 1, 1982

Most-Capped Player (65): Ivan Vicelich, 1995–

Most Goals (28): Vaughan Coveny, 1992–2007

New Zealand enters the 2010 World Cup pegged by most experts as the weakest team in the tournament, but that does nothing to inhibit the enthusiasm of the All Whites, who have qualified for only the second time in the team's history. Excellence in world soccer is not expected in New Zealand, a small and rugby-mad country, but this team is out to make the most of its opportunity, which comes as a result of winning the Oceania region and defeating Bahrain in a playoff. Success has come thanks to a connection to New Zealand's previous qualifying team: current coach Ricki Herbert played for the 1982 squad in Spain. He's been head man since 2005 and is working with a roster of largely unknown (outside New Zealand) players. One exception is Ryan Nelsen,

Rafael van der Vaart, shown here battling with Alberto Gilardino during a November 2009 friendly between Italy and Holland, and the Orange have a legitimate shot at winning it all.

team captain and central defender, who has played several years for Blackburn in the EPL. Leading scorers Shane Smeltz (Gold Coast United) and Chris Killen (Celtic) play in Australia and Scotland, respectively. Though Group F is not the toughest in South Africa, Italy is always an intimidating opponent. Yet if the Kiwis play tough against Paraguay and Slovakia, the tournament could be a memorable one for New Zealand soccer fans.

Nigeria

Population (2009): 154.7 million	
Capital: Abuja	

Nickname: Super Eagles
Qualifying Region: Africa
FIFA World Cups Hosted: None
Previous World Cup Appearances (3): 1994, 1998, 2002
Top Finish: Round of 16, 1994 and 1998
Most-Capped Player (86): Mudashiru Lawal, 1975–1985
Most Goals (37): Rashidi Yenkini, 1986–1998

Nigeria is no longer the class of African soccer, but it's not a good idea to discount a team eager to excel during the first World Cup played on its home continent. Nonetheless, experts are painting Nigeria as an underachieving team that barely qualified for the tournament. The Super Eagles earned their spot in South Africa on the merits of a come-from-behind 3–2 victory over lightly regarded Kenya in their final qualifying match, allowing them to nip Tunisia by a single point. Despite leading his team to a Cup berth, coach Shaibu Amodu was fired in February, and the job remained vacant at press time. Nigeria

is anchored defensively by two EPL stalwarts, midfielder John Obi Mikel (Chelsea) and central defender/captain Joseph Yobo (Everton). Yet Nigeria is all about offensive firepower. Ikechukwu Uche (Real Zaragoza/Spain) was the leading scorer in qualifying, but the team can field many talented goal-strikers, including Obafemi Martins (Wolfsburg), Yakubu Aiyegbeni (Everton), and Nwankwo Kanu (Portsmouth). If all this talent can gel at the right time, Nigeria has a very good chance of bettering Greece and South Korea and advancing out of Group B along with favorite Argentia.

North Korea (Korea DPR)

Population (2009): 23.9 million	
Capital: Pyongyang	

Nickname: Chollima
Qualifying Region: Asia/AFC
FIFA World Cups Hosted: None
Previous World Cup Appearances (1): 1966
Top Finish: Quarterfinals, 1966
Most-Capped Player* (48): Kim Yong-Sun
Most Goals* (12): Jong Tae-Se
*Current squad

North Korea is the mystery qualifier of World Cup 2010. It has been more than four decades since the team's last (and only) trip to the finals, and the roster includes few members who play professionally outside their home country—the most insulated nation on earth. Yet the world has had ample opportunity to see North Korea on display during the Asian region qualifying, and observers can't help but be impressed. The North Koreans finished second to South Korea in Group B with 12 points to win the automatic bid to South Africa. Once there, they may find the going a little tougher than in qualifying, but they should be competitive. Generally undersized compared to most teams, the Koreans counter this minor negative by taking a disciplined, defensive-minded approach that relies on counterattacks for offense. Head coach Kim Jong-Hun recently explained that he doesn't model his strategy on any other club but rather takes an approach that fits the players on his squad—and so far, it has worked. "We are confident about competing against the best teams in the world," Kim declared. North Korea's confidence will be tested mightily by Brazil, Portugal, and Ivory Coast in challenging Group G in South Africa.

Paraguay

Population (2009): 6.3 million	
Capital: Asuncion	

Nickname: Guarani

Qualifying Region: South America

FIFA World Cups Hosted: None

World Cup Appearances (7): 1930, 1950, 1958, 1986, 1998, 2002, 2006

Top Finish: Round 2, 1986, 1998, and 2002

Most-Capped Player (110): Carlos Gamarra, 1993–2006

Most Goals (25): Jose Saturnino Cardozo, 1991–2006

Three times Paraguay has advanced to the second round of the World Cup—most recently in 2002—but three times the team has hit the wall and advanced no further. Germany 2006 was an especially big disappointment. After bowing out in the first round, the Paraguayan Football Association hired Argentinian Gerardo Martino as manager and gave him the tough task of rebuilding a talented but aging squad. His efforts started slowly—Paraguay was routed 6–0 by Mexico in the 2007 Copa Americana—but the team gelled during World Cup qualifying, earning an early spot in South Africa on September 9, 2009, by topping Argentina 1–0. Paraguay figures to enter the world championships as the number-two South American team, outclassed by only world No. 1 Brazil. Offensively, Paraguay is keyed by the dangerous duo of Nelson Haedo Valdez (Borussia Dortmund, German Bundesliga) and Salvador Cabanas (America, Mexican Primera Division). Valdez scored the goal against Argentina that propelled his country into the World Cup. After the game he deflected praise for his score. "We play as a team, and that's more important than who scores," he explained. Then, only partly in jest, he declared, "Bring on the top dogs now!" With this type of confidence, the Guarani should advance easily out of Group F —and just might make their long-awaited breakthrough past the Round of 16 in 2010.

Portugal

Population (2009): 10.7 million

Capital: Lisbon

Nickname: Seleccao das Quinas (Selection of the Shields)

Qualifying Region: Europe/UEFA

FIFA World Cups Hosted: None

Previous World Cup Appearances (4): 1966, 1986, 2002, 2006

Top Finish: Third Place, 1966

Most-Capped Player (127): Luis Figo, 1991–2006

Most Goals (47): Pauleta, 1997–2006

That Portugal was one of the last teams to qualify for the 2010 World Cup—and until late in UEFA qualifying appeared destined to sit out the tournament—is amazing. Coming off a fourth-place finish in Germany 2006 and boasting a talent-rich roster (including superstar Cristiano Ronaldo), the Portuguese started qualifying among the favorites to win it all in 2010. After winning just one of its first five qualifying matches, Portugal righted the ship and nipped Sweden for second place in UEFA Group One, then beat Bosnia-Herzegovina in a playoff for the Cup berth. Coach Carlos Queiroz—previously the head man for host South Africa—will have no lack of talent to call on, but Ronaldo will be the key to his team. The Real Madrid superstar striker will be supported offensively by Simao Sabrosa (Atletico Madrid), the leading scorer in qualifying, Deco (Chelsea), and Raul Meireles (Porto). Even with this star power on attack, the team's real strength may be along the back line. The Chelsea duo of Ricardo Carvalho and Jose Bosingwa along with Pepe (Real Madrid) and Bruno Alves (Porto) makes the Portuguese one of the toughest to score on. With its recent improved performance, Portugal's primary concern heading to South Africa will be a tough draw: Group G will likely be dominated by Brazil, but Ivory Coast will challenge Portugal for the other spot in the Round of 16.

Serbia

Population (2009): 7.3 million

Capital: Belgrade

Nickname: Beli Orlovi (White Eagles)

Qualifying Region: Europe/UEFA

FIFA World Cups Hosted: None

Previous World Cup Appearances (10): 1930, 1950, 1954, 1958, 1962, 1974, 1982, 1990, 1998, 2006

Top Finish: Fourth Place, 1930 and 1962

Most-Capped Player (102): Savo Milosevic, 1994–2008

Most Goals (37): Savo Milosevic, 1994–2008

Serbia has only been an independent nation since 2006, and technically 2010 will be its first World Cup, but FIFA recognizes the nation as the rightful heir to the soccer heritage and record of Yugoslavia and Serbia and Montenegro. The 2006 Cup was a huge disappointment for the Serbian-dominated S and M squad. It went to Germany undefeated in qualifying yet failed to win a game at the tournament. Serbia goes to South Africa as winner of UEFA Group Seven, having left perennial power France in the dust as runner-up. In fact, Serbia's biggest problem in qualifying may have been its fans, whose bad behavior earned the country fines and threats of a points deduction. The

The most expensive player in soccer history, Cristiano Ronaldo was sold to Real Madrid in 2009 for a record $132 million. Looking to rebound after his 2006 World Cup ended in disappointment, Ronaldo and his Portuguese teammates will have to navigate through either Brazil or Ivory Coast to advance.

key to the team's success has been the leadership of veteran coach Radomir Antic, who emerged from semiretirement to take over the club in 2008. On the pitch, striker Milan Jovanovic (Standard Liege, Belgium) was the team's top scorer during qualifying. The defense is led by two rising stars in the EPL, Branislav Ivanovic of Chelsea and Nemanja Vidic of Manchester United. The captain, unquestioned leader, and most versatile midfielder is veteran Dejan Stankovic of Inter Milan. With this core of world-class talent, Serbia looks like a worthy heir to the rich Yugoslavian soccer tradition and a favorite to advance out of Group D to the Round of 16, and maybe beyond, in South Africa.

Slovakia

Population (2008): 5.4 million	
Capital: Bratislava	

Nickname: Bonjovni Jondovci (The Fighting Jondas)

Qualifying Region: Europe/UEFA

FIFA World Cups Hosted: None

Previous World Cup Appearances: None

Top Finish: N/A

Most-Capped Player (93): Miroslav Karhan, 1995–

Most Goals (22): Szilard Nemeth, 1996–

Slovakia became an independent nation on January 1, 1993, after the peaceful dissolution of the former Czechoslovakia, and made its first attempt at World Cup qualification for the 1998 tournament. After falling short three times, Slovakia qualified for the 2010 tournament by winning UEFA Group Three with 22 points. The Slovakians are coached by Vladimir Weiss—the middle generation

of a three era Slovakian soccer family all with the same name. Grandfather Vladimir Weiss made three appearances for the Czechoslovakian national team, while grandson Vladimir Weiss is a midfielder for Manchester City and a regular in the same position on the national team. There are few household names on the Slovakian team, but they played well in winning a tough group, tallying 22 goals in 10 games. Leading scorer Stanislav Sestak (six goals in qualifying) plays for VfL Bochum in the Bundesliga. Six-foot-three-inch defender Martin Skrtel (Liverpool) towers over a back line that plays hard-nosed defense. Slovakia's mix of scoring prowess, stingy defending, and strong team play will surely make them a dark-horse contender heading into South Africa. Their competition for second place in Group F will be Paraguay, with Italy the clear favorite to take the top spot.

Slovenia

Population (2009): 2.0 million	
Capital: Ljubljana	

Nickname: N/A

Qualifying Region: Europe/UEFA

FIFA World Cups Hosted: None

World Cup Appearances (1): 2002

Top Finish: Round 1, 2002

Most-Capped Player (80): Zlatko Zahovic, 1992–2004

Most Goals (35): Zlatko Zahovic, 1992–2004

Slovenia declared its independence from the crumbling Yugoslavia in 1991, played its first international soccer match a year later, and entered World Cup qualifying for the 1998 tournament. Unsuccessful the first time out, Slovenia earned a spot in Japan/South Korea in 2002 but bowed out quickly after three first-round losses. The country is hungry for a chance to better this record— a realistic goal thanks to the team's punishing defense, which yielded only four goals in 10 UEFA Group Three qualifying matches. Yet Slovenia nearly missed out on a trip to South Africa after finishing second to Slovakia and drawing a strong Russian squad in the playoffs. The home-and-home series ended even at 2–2, but a single away goal by Slovenia proved the difference. The Slovenians are lacking big-name stars, but their roster is dotted with quality. Key players include: striker Milivoje Novakovic (Cologne), far and away the team's leading scorer; keeper Samir Handanovic, who plays in Italy's Serie A with Udinese; and team captain Robert Koren, midfielder for English Championship squad West Bromich Albion. Advancing out of Group C ahead of England and the U.S. will be a challenge, but they should pose a serious challenge for those larger soccer powers.

South Africa

Population (2009): 49.3 million

Capital: Pretoria (administrative seat)

Nickname: Bafana Bafana (The Boys)

Qualifying Region: Hosts

FIFA World Cups Hosted (1): 2010

Previous World Cup Appearances (2): 1998, 2002

Top Finish: Round 1, 1998 and 2002

Most-Capped Player (90): Aaron Mokoena, 1999–

Most Goals (31): Benni McCarthy, 1997–

During its era of Apartheid, South Africa was an exile from the World Cup, but now it is proudly hosting the tournament. Since its re-entry starting in 1994, the county has established itself as a quality participant on the world stage, but 2010 offers an exciting opportunity to elevate its reputation even more. Like previous hosts, the team is determined to prove it is worthy of its free pass into one of the 32 precious spots. In 2009 South Africa made a strong statement about its legitimacy by finishing fourth in a very competitive Confederations Cup, losing a hard-fought 1–0 match in the semifinals. Then in the third-place match against Spain, "The Boys" forced the game into extra time before losing 3–2. Well-traveled Brazilian Joel Santana manages the team. It's his first international team assignment, but clearly he has his team prepared to take on the world's best. South Africa's most exciting player is undoubtedly Teko Modise, the active goal leader (assuming that Benni McCarthy is not brought back for 2010) with 11 scores. The 26-year-old winger is still playing at home with the Orlando Pirates, but his name has been linked with top clubs in England and Italy. Adding a stable, mature influence is midfielder Aaron Mokoena (Portsmouth, EPL). The 31-year-old South African captain will provide a physical defensive presence that Bafana Bafana will need if they hope to advance beyond the initial round for the first time in the country's short World Cup history.

South Korea

Population (2009): 48.4 million

Capital: Seoul

Nickname: Taeguk Warriors

Qualifying Region: Asia/AFC

FIFA World Cups Hosted (1): 2002 (co-hosted with Japan)

Previous World Cup Appearances (7): 1954, 1986, 1990, 1994, 1998, 2002, 2006

Top Finish: Fourth Place, 2002

Most-Capped Player (136): Hong Myung-Bo, 1990–2002

Most Goals (55): Cha Burn-Kun, 1972–1986

Asian soccer doesn't get as much credit as it deserves, but the team that has done the most to change the status quo is South Korea. By winning Asian Group B with 16 points, the Taeguk Warriors booked their seventh consecutive trip to the finals. The country's shining moment in the tournament came in 2002 when, as co-host with Japan, it made a surprising yet determined run to a fourth-place finish. Can the 2010 team match this heady achievement? It's hard to say, and South Korea's recent performance has been inconsistent, but South Africa might be the last opportunity for the outstanding players who emerged in the 2002 Cup. Captain and international superstar Park Ji-sung (he plays midfield for Manchester United) has already announced that 2010 will be his last World Cup, even though he'll be a relatively young 29 at tournament time. "I don't think my stamina will last until the next one in 2014," he explained shortly after South Korea clinched its South Africa berth. Coach Huh Jung-Moo—in his third stint leading the team—may need younger players to step forward if the club wants to move beyond the first round. Lee Chung-Yong, already playing with EPL side Bolton Wanderers at the tender age of 21, is a likely candidate for international stardom. The Under-20 World Cup in 2007 was his coming-out party, he made his premiere with the senior squad in May 2008, and he scored his first international goal in a qualifying match against Jordan just three months later.

Spain

Population (2009): 46.7 million

Capital: Madrid

Nickname: La Furia Roja (The Red Fury)

Qualifying Region: Europe/UEFA

FIFA World Cups Hosted (1): 1982

World Cup Appearances (12): 1934, 1950, 1962, 1966, 1978, 1982, 1986, 1990, 1994, 1998, 2002, 2006

Top Finish: Fourth Place, 1950

Most-Capped Player (126): Andoni Zubizarreta, 1985–1998

Most Goals (44): Raul Gonzalez, 1996–

Spain is the only team that has earned a FIFA No. 1 ranking without ever having won a World Cup. The fact that this soccer-mad country—home to maybe the world's top professional league—has never finished higher than fourth in the world championships is perplexing, but that record may change in South Africa. Spain's current team is deeply talented, as evidenced by its victory in Euro 2008 that earned the No. 1 ranking. A managerial switch after that tournament, with Vincente del Bosque replacing Luis Aragones, didn't slow the team one bit. They reeled off 15 straight victories under the new skipper, a string ended by a

The electrifying David Villa is just one of many weapons on a loaded Spain team that ranks number one in the world but suffered a disappointing loss to the United States at the 2009 Confederations Cup.

semifinal loss to the U.S. in the 2009 Confederations Cup—but even that stumble looks to be a minor one. Valencia star David Villa has emerged as the squad's top goal scorer. He logged a Spain calendar-year record of 12 scores in 2008, though fellow striker Fernando Torres (Liverpool) and winger Andres Iniesta (Barcelona) are equal threats to put the ball in the net. Defensively, Spain is also one of the world's top teams, with Barcelona's Carles Puyol anchoring the back line and team captain Iker Casillas patrolling the goalmouth. Many consider the Real Madrid player the world's finest goalkeeper. With its talent, recent record of success, and drive to bring home the Cup for the first time, Spain must be considered one of the favorites to win the tournament in South Africa.

Switzerland

Population (2009): 7.7 million	
Capital: Bern	

Nickname: Schweizer Nati

Qualifying Region: Europe/UEFA

FIFA World Cups Hosted (1): 1954

Previous World Cup Appearances (8): 1934, 1938, 1950, 1954, 1962, 1966, 1994, 2006

Top Finish: Quarterfinals, 1934, 1938, and 1954

Most-Capped Player (117): Heinz Hermann, 1978–1991

Most Goals (40): Alexander Frei, 2001–

Switzerland is playing in the World Cup finals for the ninth time, but it has been more than a half century since the country has been considered among soccer's elite teams. In 2006, the Swiss never yielded a goal yet were eliminated in the Round of 16 by Romania—on penalty kicks after a scoreless draw. Switzerland left Germany determined to re-establish its credentials but started slowly in UEFA qualifying for 2010, posting a draw and a loss to open the competition. Then the Swiss caught fire, winning five straight matches en route to the top spot in Group Two. With this strong finish comes an upsurge in optimism for South Africa. Coach Otttmar Hitzfeld's squad nicely blends experience and youth. Captain and all-time leading scorer Alexander Frei (FC Basel, Switzerland) has played on the Swiss team since 2001. His attacking partner up front, Blaise N'Kufo (FC Twente, Netherlands), has won fewer caps but earned his first in 2002. Talented younger players such as midfielder Tranquillo Barnetta (Bayer Leverkusen) and goalkeeper Diego Benaglio (Wolfsburg) add energy and nicely complement the veterans. Group H should provide some exciting matches come June, but Switzerland has to be counted with Spain as a favorite to advance to the Round of 16—and maybe deeper into the tournament.

One of the top defensive teams in the world, Switzerland did not yield a goal outside of extra-time penalty kicks in its last World Cup appearance. The Swiss tenacity makes them a favorite to advance from Group H along with Spain.

Uruguay

Population (2009): 3.4 million

Capital: Montevideo

Nickname: Charruas

Qualifying Region: South America/CONMEBOL

FIFA World Cups Hosted (1): 1930

Previous World Cup Appearances (10): 1930, 1950, 1954, 1962, 1966, 1970, 1974, 1986, 1990, 2002

Championships (2): 1930, 1950

Most-Capped Player (79): Rodolfo Rodriguez, 1976–1986

Most Goals (31): Hector Scarone, 1917–1930

Today, Uruguay is lightly regarded among soccer powers, but the country hosted and won the first World Cup (in 1930), won a second time 20 years later, and remained a regular qualifier and championship contender through 1990. For the 2010 Cup, Uruguay snuck into the final 32 by the slimmest of margins: they lost to Argentina and conceded the last automatic spot in South America but defeated Costa Rica 2–1 (on aggregate) in a playoff between the CONMEBOL/CONCACAF almost-qualifiers. Manager Oscar Washington Tabarez is on his second stint leading Uruguay. He coached the team to its 1990 Round of 16 appearance—at the time a disappointing result that led to his dismissal. This time around he has an offensively potent squad—the team tallied 28 goals in qualifying games. Dangerous strikers Diego Forlan (Atletico Madrid) and Luis Suarez (Ajax) combined for 12 scores. The 30-year-old Forlan played on Uruguay's last World Cup squad (2002), while Suarez is just 22 and a relative newcomer to the national team. Manning the central defense is team captain Diego Lugano, a fan favorite with top Turkish side Fenerbahce. Despite almost not qualifying, Uruguay will not be taken lightly by its opponents in South Africa and should make a strong run at the Round of 16 in a wide-open, evenly matched Group A.

Uruguay forward Luis Suarez (right) chases down Argentina's star forward Lionel Messi during their FIFA World Cup South Africa 2010 qualifier match at the Centenario Stadium in Montevideo in October 2009.

The U.S. Men's
NATIONAL TEAM

There was a time when playing soccer for the U.S. Men's National Team was really not that great of an achievement. That time is long past. With the team boasting appearances in five straight World Cups, a slot on the final roster of 23 names is highly coveted, and the competition to achieve this goal is fierce.

The road to establishing the final roster for the 2010 World Cup began in earnest in early 2007 and included a lot more than just 23 players. At all times, U.S. Soccer maintains a player pool of individuals eligible for inclusion on the game rosters. At the start of the 2009 qualification round, 52 players were included in the pool, broken down by position in the following way: 7 goalkeepers, 19 defenders, 19 midfielders, and 7 forwards. The pool is always changing, for obvious reasons—players retire, injuries take their toll, and new talent emerges from the U.S.'s highly successful youth teams. The pool is an interesting mix of well-known and somewhat obscure names; all are playing professionally for clubs around the world. Nearly half of the pool is playing at home in the MLS, but teams from a dozen other countries are represented.

Bob Bradley and the coaching staff used 2007 to take a look at a generous slice of American soccer talent. In fact, 72 names made up the 2007 pool, and 61 players appeared with the Men's National Team that year; 23 of those individuals were earning their first "cap." (The term is rooted in soccer's early days when players were actually given a cap as a token of remembrance for playing on their country's national team.) The international tryout did not go well for many players—16 earned but a single cap—but the process allowed the coaches to better hone their team for the World Cup CONCACAF qualification round that began in 2008.

In 2008 Bradley used only 46 different players on his squad, and as 2009 dawned, Bradley had focused in on a group that seemed to be the favorites for a roster slot the following year. Yet, over the course of 2009, things changed dramatically. Key players were victimized by injuries, and others who had missed time with various ailments returned to form. In addition, new players were added to the mix, and some responded with such strong play that they forced their way into the lineup. As a result, the starting 11 (plus substitutes) for the final qualifier, on October 14, 2009, against Costa Rica, looked like this:

Defenders Carlos Bocanegra and Oguchi Onyewu battle the Brazilians at the 2009 Confederations Cup. If the U.S. can advance past the first round of the World Cup, they might get another crack at Brazil, which should be the pre-tournament favorite.

G: Tim Howard
D: Steve Cherundolo
D: Carlos Bocanegra (captain)
D: Oguchi Onyewu
D: Jonathan Bornstein
M: Stuart Holden (sub: Robbie Rogers, 69)
M: Michael Bradley
M: Benny Feilhaber (sub: Jose Francisco Torres, 63)
M: Landon Donovan
F: Jozy Altidore
F: Conor Casey (Kenny Cooper, 79)

With the exception of two midfield positions—with Clint Dempsey and Ricardo Clark replacing Holden and Feilhaber, respectively—this could very well be the team that takes the field against England come June.

A quick analysis of the various positions reveals some areas of confidence and other areas with question marks looming:

Goalkeepers: This is an area of strength for the U.S., with Tim Howard starting and the very capable Brad Guzan backing him up. Plus, if Howard is lost to injury, it's not a stretch to imagine the U.S. coaxing the still-excellent Brad Friedel out of international retirement.

Defenders: This position is loaded with talent but has been ravaged by injuries. Oguchi Onyewu is the best but is a question mark as he recovers from a patellar tendon rupture. Jonathan Bornstein and Steve Cherundolo finally appear to be healthy but have missed considerable playing time in recent years. The same goes for Jay DeMerit and Jonathan Spector. Carlos Bocanegra has been healthy, but his play has not been his best over the past year. The ageless and energetic Frankie Hedjuk may be called on as an insurance policy, and Chad Marshall might emerge as a starter if the injury bug hits again.

Midfielders: This is an area of strength but is also unsettled. If Clint Dempsey is healthy, count on him starting alongside Landon Donovan, Michael Bradley, and Ricardo Clark (who also was injured over the winter). Or will Bob Bradley play Dempsey as a striker and start the emerging Stuart Holden on the right wing? Will DaMarcus Beasley's recent strong play put him back in the mix? Is Clark really the answer as a holding midfielder? Benny Feilhaber and young Jose Francisco Torres both have supporters who feel that they would be a better option.

Forwards: Jozy Altidore appears to have cemented his role as a starter, but who will anchor the spot beside him? Last summer, the U.S. looked to have found the answer in the form of Charlie Davies, but his rehab from injuries likely won't be complete by the start of the Cup. Clint Dempsey can be moved up front, but the more physical veterans Conor Casey and Brian Ching might be safer options, leaving Dempsey free to attack from the right wing. Other strikers—including Jeff Cunningham and Kenny Cooper—may get a long look in the run-up to the tournament.

Charlie Davies was a dynamic contributor during the qualification stretch run in 2009 but injuries suffered in a car accident make him a doubtful participant in South Africa.

United States
PLAYER PROFILES

Landon Donovan

Position: Attacking midfielder/striker

Height: 5'8" • Weight: 150

Date of Birth: March 4, 1982

Hometown: Redlands, California

Professional Club: L.A. Galaxy

Landon Donovan is only 28, but he has starred on the U.S. men's team for a decade. He has tallied 42 goals and 42 assists (No. 1 all-time in both categories) during his career, yet he still has his detractors. South Africa may provide the ultimate opportunity for Donovan to prove them wrong.

Growing up in southern California, Donovan's talent was evident from when he started playing soccer at the age of six. He was a member of the first class at the IMG Soccer Academy, and in 1999 was named the top player at the FIFA U-17 World Cup. The next year he starred for the U.S. Olympic team and made his first international appearance for the senior team.

Donovan scored two goals and was named Best Young Player in the 2002 World Cup, but four later took much of the criticism for the U.S. stumbles in Germany. In addition, Donovan's mixed record on the club level hurt his reputation. Despite becoming MLS's biggest star, playing for the San Jose Earthquakes (2001–2005) and the L.A. Galaxy (since 2005) and scoring nearly 100 goals, he failed on repeated attempts to break into the German Bundesliga. And then there was Donovan's role in the highly publicized David Beckham saga, going public with his negative feelings about his new teammate in a book written by Grant Wahl.

Yet amidst this backdrop Donovan put together one of the best years of his career in 2009. In World Cup qualifying, he was consistently the U.S. team's best—and hardest-working—player. Back home, he sealed his rift with Beckham and led the Galaxy to the MLS Cup Final.

The year 2010 promises to be an even better one for Donovan. After signing a contract extension with the Galaxy, he was given one last opportunity to redeem himself in Europe on a 10-week loan to Everton of the EPL. He responded by quickly establishing himself as one of the most exciting players in the world's top league—giving notice that he was ready for even bigger things come June, in South Africa.

Years	Caps	Starts	Minutes	Goals	Assists	Yellow	Red
2000–2009	120	108	9,901	42	42	11	0

Jozy Altidore

Position: Forward • Height: 6'1"

Weight: 175

Date of Birth: November 6, 1989

Hometown: Boca Raton, Florida

Professional Club: Hull City (England)

Even while Freddy Adu was grabbing all the headlines, another American teenager was flashing his remarkable soccer skills and giving U.S. fans hope for the future. Josmer "Jozy" Altidore, a New Jersey native born to Haitian parents, was the 17th pick in the 2006 MLS SuperDraft and became a key contributor to the New York Red Bulls playoff run later that season. In fact, the 16-year-old Altidore became the youngest player to start and score in an MLS playoff game.

It was only a matter of time before Europe came calling. On June 4, 2008, Villareal signed an MLS-record transfer fee of $10 million for the chance to showcase Altidore in Spain. The youngster appeared in a half-dozen games, scoring a single goal, but playing time was hard to come by on the talent-laden squad. A loan to Spanish second-division club Xerex for the remainder of the 2008–2009 season also left Altidore sitting on the bench. Fortunately, a new opportunity presented itself in the summer of 2009.

English Premier League club Hull City eagerly signed Altidore to a season-long loan agreement for 2009–2010. The deal reportedly provided an option to make the deal permanent at the end of the campaign. The young American provided the shot in the arm Hull desired almost instantly, setting up the winning goal mere seconds after entering his first game for the team. At press time, he had scored just two goals for Hull but at least was getting regular playing time.

Altidore has enjoyed more success on the international stage, often pairing with Freddy Adu to form a deadly offensive force for U.S. youth teams. Altidore scored three goals during the successful U-20 World Cup in 2007, including both scores during a 2–1 victory over Brazil. Shortly after Altidore turned 18 in November 2007, Bob Bradley gave him his first taste of senior-team action when he came on as a sub against South Africa. Altidore started his first U.S. MNT game, a friendly against Mexico, in February 2008, and also tallied his first international goal in that game.

Altidore established himself as a key U.S. player during the 2009 World Cup qualifying campaign, starting with the game in El Salvador. His aggressive play as a substitute and brilliant goal off a header helped the U.S. salvage a draw. Minor toe surgery slowed him in the spring, but Altidore rebounded nicely at the Confederations Cup, where his physical presence caused problems for some of the world's top defenders. His brilliant goal in the win over Spain was Altidore's best moment to date as a U.S. team member—hopefully he will enjoy similar highlights in South Africa.

Years	Caps	Starts	Minutes	Goals	Assists	Yellow	Red
2007–2009	23	3	1,428	8	2	4	0

Carlos Bocanegra

Position: Defender

Height: 6' • Weight: 170

Date of Birth: May 25, 1979

Hometown: Alta Loma, California

Professional Club: Stade Rennais (France)

Carlos Bocanegra has quietly emerged as one of the most important players on the U.S. Men's National Team, serving as captain, anchoring the defense, and providing leadership that keeps his younger teammates focused on the task at hand. On the club level, he has enjoyed success in both the U.S. and Europe. The California native honed his skills during three seasons at UCLA before moving to the MLS Chicago Fire in 2000. Bocanegra earned MLS Rookie of the Year honors and played a key role in Chicago's march to an MLS Cup title. He followed that up by being named MLS Defender of the Year in both 2002 and 2003.

Bocanegra was signed by Fulham of the English Premiership in January 2004 and for three seasons was a fixture on a definitely American-flavored squad led by forward Brian McBride. Bocanegra was released by Fulham at the end of 2008 but quickly signed with French club Stade Rennais. There he helped Rennes climb near the top of the Ligue 1 standings and was voted "sexiest player" by a poll of the team's supporters! Unfortunately, his playing time decreased early in 2009–2010, but at press time he had returned to the starting lineup.

Bocanegra's rise on the international stage came at a slower pace. Though he made his U.S. MNT debut in late 2001 and was a frequent starter over the next few years, he wasn't always Bruce Arena's first choice on the back line. Current coach Bob Bradley had more confidence in Bocanegra, and he has played in almost every important U.S. game over the past four years, either at center or left back and typically wearing the captain's armband. Bocanegra is dangerous in the air, which has helped him tally 10 international goals, but tough defense is his trademark. His deceptive speed, aggressive tackling, and cool head give his teammates tremendous confidence.

Years	Caps	Starts	Minutes	Goals	Assists	Yellow	Red
2001–2009	76	72	6,022	11	7	18	1

Jonathan Bornstein

Position: Defender	
Height: 5'9" • Weight: 145	
Date of Birth: November 7, 1984	
Hometown: Los Alamitos, California	
Professional Club: Chivas USA	

Though his international career has been hampered by injuries, Jonathan Bornstein over the past three years has proven himself to be the U.S. team's best option at left back when he's healthy. Though small in stature, Bornstein is both fast and hard working and his availability for much of 2009 is one of the reasons the American team qualified for the 2010 World Cup.

A graduate of UCLA, the California native has also made his mark on the professional level in his home state. Drafted by Chivas USA in 2006, he became a starter for the team his first season and was named MLS Rookie of the Year. In his second season he was named to MLS Best XI.

In January 2007 Bornstein made his first international appearance, against Denmark, and even scored a goal in the game. He soon became a starter and favorite of U.S. coach Bob Bradley—also his first coach at Chivas USA. Though bitten by the injury bug in 2008 and early 2009, Bornstein eventually worked himself back into shape and won back the starting position that he'd given up to Heath Pearce. Going into South Africa—with the health of other U.S. defenders in doubt—it is clear that only an injury will keep Bornstein out of the lineup. His prowess at stopping speedy wingers and ability to push forward offensively will be keys to U.S. success at World Cup 2010.

Years	Caps	Starts	Minutes	Goals	Assists	Yellow	Red
2007–2009	26	23	2,050	2	0	6	0

Michael Bradley

Position: Midfielder

Height: 6'2" • Weight: 175

Date of Birth: July 31, 1987

Hometown: Manhattan Beach, California

Professional Club: Borussia Monchengladbach (Germany)

Though it doesn't hurt that his father, Bob, is the coach of the U.S. Men's National Team, Michael Bradley has relied on talent rather than nepotism to secure a spot in the lineup. The fact that this exciting young midfielder is also making a big mark in the German Bundesliga is evidence of his exceptional skills.

Bradley was born in New Jersey while his father was coach at Princeton, and he emerged as a youth soccer phenom in the Chicago suburbs while the elder Bradley coached the MLS Fire. The younger Bradley turned professional when he was only 16. He was selected by the New York/New Jersey MetroStars in the 2004 MLS SuperDraft but because of injury did not play until 2005, when he appeared in 30 games.

In 2006 Bradley moved to Heerenveen of the Dutch first division, in the process becoming the youngest player ever sold by MLS. He enjoyed a breakout season in 2007–2008, starting 30 matches and scoring 16 goals in league competition, which led to a four-year contract with Bundesliga side Borussian Mochengladbach. By the second half of the 2008–2009 season, Bradley had became a regular in the starting lineup.

Bradley saw his first U.S. MNT minutes thanks to former coach Bruce Arena, who used him as a sub in warm-up games before the 2006 World Cup. Bradley started his first senior international game in 2007 after his father had assumed the U.S. helm. He started 11 games for the U.S. in 2008 and in 2009 reinforced his importance to the squad by scoring both goals in the decisive February victory over Mexico. The only blotch on his 2009 record was a controversial red card in the Confederations Cup victory over Spain that kept him out of the tournament final. Fortunately, Bradley should have ample opportunity to redeem himself on the world stage in 2010.

Years	Caps	Starts	Minutes	Goals	Assists	Yellow	Red
2006–2009	40	36	3,158	7	0	9	2

Conor Casey

Position: Forward

Height: 6'1" • Weight: 170

Date of Birth: July 25, 1981

Hometown: Gilpin, Colorado

Professional Club: Colorado Rapids

In an unlikely turn of events, Conor Casey emerged as a key contributor for the U.S. in 2009, as well as the hero of the team's October qualifier in Honduras. His inspired play and two goals contributed to the victory that clinched a spot in South Africa. Not exactly the most elegant or speedy player, Casey relies on hard work and a physical presence to make an impact.

This has been a pleasant development for a player whose soccer career seemed on life support just a couple of years earlier. Casey grew up in Colorado and played for the University of Portland, but he left school after two seasons to try his luck as a professional in Germany. He bounced around among four clubs over six seasons, finally settling with Mainz 05, but was released following an injury-marred tenure. Casey returned to the States and MLS, playing briefly with Toronto before landing back home in Colorado. With the Rapids, he's played in 60 games over three seasons, scoring 29 goals. His 16 strikes in 2009 were second best in MLS.

After a smattering of appearances for the U.S. in 2004 and 2005, Casey was dropped from the player pool thanks to his injuries. His MLS play caught Bob Bradley's attention, and he finally made his mark in 2009, appearing in seven games and starting four. With the U.S. short on strikers because of the Charlie Davies injury, it is likely that Casey will see a lot of playing time during the 2010 World Cup.

Years	Caps	Starts	Minutes	Goals	Assists	Yellow	Red
2004-2009	17	9	n/a	2	0	0	0

Steve Cherundolo

Position: Defender

Height: 5'6" • Weight: 145

Date of Birth: February 19, 1979

Hometown: San Diego, California

Professional Club: Hannover 96 (Germany)

Short and speedy, Steve Cherundolo is unique among soccer players for having played for a single club during his 11-year professional career—Hannover 96 of the German Bundesliga. When Cherundolo is healthy, there is probably nobody Bob Bradley would rather have manning the right-back position, but health has been an issue throughout the defender's career. In fact, as 2009 international play started, he was recovering from a hip injury and unavailable for U.S. MNT action, though he recovered in time take the captain's role on a young CONCACAF Gold Cup team that finished second to Mexico.

Cherundolo grew up in California and played for the University of Portland before turning pro in 1999. He signed with Hannover 96 when they were a second-division club. His first year as a regular starter, 2001–2002, coincided with the team's rise to the top of the league and promotion to the Bundesliga. Hannover 96 has maintained its top-flight status ever since.

Cherundolo made his U.S. senior team debut in 1999 and was a late addition to the 2002 World Cup roster, though an injury kept him out of the tournament. He received another opportunity four years later, appearing in all three World Cup games in Germany. If Cherundolo can stay fit in 2010, he'll be a likely starter when the U.S. opens World Cup play.

Years	Caps	Starts	Minutes	Goals	Assists	Yellow	Red
1999–2009	57	55	4,432	2	8	9	1

Ricardo Clark

Position: Midfielder

Height: 5'10" • Weight: 150

Date of Birth: February 10, 1983

Hometown: Jonesboro, Georgia

Professional Club: Eintracht Frankfurt (Germany)

The year 2009 was a breakout for Ricardo Clark's international career. After four years of sporadic appearances on the U.S. team, Clark became Bob Bradley's first choice as holding midfielder during the CONCACAF qualifying cycle. He and Michael Bradley complement each other well in the midfield. The pair put on a particularly impressive show against Spain in the Confederations Cup semifinal.

The Georgia native played two years of college ball at Furman, then jumped to the MLS MetroStars, where he was a finalist for the 2003 Rookie of the Year. A 2005 trade to San Jose (which moved to Houston in 2006) didn't slow him one bit, and he was a key player for the club's 2006 MLS Cup run. With his superlative play in 2009, both for the Dynamo and the U.S., Clark earned a chance to ply his trade in Europe. He was signed by Eintracht Frankfurt of the Bundesliga, but at press time he had yet to play his first game.

The defensive-minded Clark scored just a single goal for the U.S. in 2009, but it was a big one—the only score in the American team's tough 1–0 September win on the road against Trinidad & Tobago. He won't be called on to score in South Africa, but the U.S. will need Clark to be playing the best soccer of his life if it wants to compete with the world's top teams.

Years	Caps	Starts	Minutes	Goals	Assists	Yellow	Red
2005–2009	27	21	1,861	2	1	2	1

Clint Dempsey

Position: Attacking midfielder/forward

Height: 6'1" • Weight: 170

Date of Birth: March 9, 1983

Hometown: Nacogdoches, Texas

Professional Club: Fulham (England)

Landon Donovan may get more headlines, but Clint Dempsey is probably the most gifted soccer player on the U.S. team—the one undeniable talent capable of turning the course of a game with a single brilliant move. He did this repeatedly in 2009, most notably at the Confederations Cup, where he earned the Bronze Ball as the third-best player at the tournament. It is difficult to imagine a strong U.S. run at the 2010 World Cup without Dempsey—which is why U.S. fans everywhere were stunned when they heard about his January knee injury, suffered playing for Fulham. At press time, the news was positive; damage was minimal, and Dempsey was expected to be ready for South Africa, eliciting a collective sigh of relief from American supporters.

The initial consternation caused by Dempsey's injury is ironic considering that, despite his brilliance, he is one of the most-maligned members of the U.S. team. His tendency to make silly mistakes and to go long stretches of games without contributing much can be extremely frustrating, but Dempsey's passion to win, toughness, and his ability to strike out of the blue makes him a must-have player.

Ironically, Dempsey has been anything but inconsistent as a club player. The Texas native joined the New England Revolution after three years at Furman University, earned MLS Rookie of the Year honors in 2004, and was named MLS Best XI in 2005. He moved to Fulham in January 2007 for a then-MLS-record transfer fee of $4 million and became a starter for the London club the next season. With 20 goals scored in his short career, Dempsey has established himself as one of the EPL's most exciting offensive players, and his play earned him a contract extension through 2013. Fans on both sides of the Atlantic are crossing their fingers that he makes a full and fast recovery this spring.

Years	Caps	Starts	Minutes	Goals	Assists	Yellow	Red
2004–2009	60	52	4,437	17	7	2	0

Tim Howard

Position: Goalkeeper

Height: 6'3" • **Weight:** 210

Date of Birth: March 6, 1979

Hometown: North Brunswick, New Jersey

Professional Club: Everton (England)

The latest in a long line of outstanding U.S. goalkeepers, Tim Howard is a fitting heir to a great tradition. Athletic, intelligent, and passionate, Howard is a vocal force in the American net, constantly yelling instructions and encouragement but also giving teammates confidence knowing that he will usually be in the right place at the right time should defensive plans go awry.

Howard's personal journey to the top of the soccer world is an inspiring one. The New Jersey native overcame his parents' divorce, racism (he is of mixed-race heritage), and Tourette syndrome (which causes uncontrollable tics and vocal outbursts) thanks to his involvement in sports. He excelled at both basketball and soccer—in both midfield and in goal—but soccer was clearly his future. He was in the goal for U.S. youth teams by the age of 15, played his first professional game (for New Jersey of the USISL) before he graduated from high school, and started his first MLS game, for the MetroStars, when he was 19.

After 88 MLS appearances, Howard received a stunning call-up to the big time in 2003 when Manchester United acquired him and made him its starter. His first years in the EPL were a mixed bag. Though he was named to the EPL Best XI for 2003–2004 and became the first American to play for the winning side in an FA Cup final, Howard also had occasional lapses that affected his confidence and eventually put him on the bench. He signed a new contract with Man U in 2006 but was clearly not in the team's long-term plans. A 2006–2007 loan to Everton turned into a permanent transfer the following season, and Howard has used the fresh opportunity to establish himself as one of the EPL's top keepers.

On the international level, Howard had to wait his turn behind Brad Friedel and Kasey Keller (whom he backed up for the 2006 World Cup), but he became the American team's first-choice keeper after the latter's retirement. His play since then has been outstanding, highlighted by being named the best goalkeeper at the 2009 Confederations Cup. Howard will undoubtedly be a key player if the U.S. hopes to make a strong run at the 2010 World Cup.

Years	Caps	Starts	Minutes	Goals	Assists	Yellow	Red
2002–2009	50	47	4,005	42	19	0	0

Oguchi Onyewu

Position: Defender	
Height: 6'4" • Weight: 210	
Date of Birth: May 13, 1982	
Hometown: Olney, Maryland	
Professional Club: AC Milan (Italy)	

When Oguchi Onyewu crumpled to the ground in the October qualifier against Costa Rica with what turned out to be a ruptured patellar tendon, some fans feared that the death knell for the U.S. team's hopes in South Africa had been sounded. The towering defender had become the rock of the U.S. back line, a cool customer who could be relied upon to clear danger from in front of the net. Plus, the timing of the injury couldn't have been worse for Onyewu's club career—he had recently been signed by Italian power AC Milan and was competing for playing time. Would this sidetrack his quest for success?

Fortunately, the news about Onyewu at press time was positive. With his injury rehabilitation progressing nicely, U.S. team officials were confident that he would be ready for South Africa, though his match fitness will be another matter.

Onyewu was born in the U.S. to Nigerian parents who had relocated to Washington, D.C., to attend college. He is a product of the U.S. residency program at the IMG Soccer Academy and played two years of soccer at Clemson before signing with Metz of the French Ligue 1 in 2002. Loans to two Belgian clubs led to a permanent transfer to Standard Liege starting in 2004–2005, and he was named as one of Belgium's Best XI that season. A short-lived, poor-quality showing on loan to Newcastle in 2007 sent Onyewu back to Standard Liege, but he was again among Belgium's best the following two seasons, leading to the contract with AC Milan.

Onyewu has been a mainstay on the U.S. team for several years, having started all three games in the 2006 World Cup and most of the games during the recent qualifying process for South Africa. Bob Bradley and the rest of the American team are undoubtedly crossing their fingers that this exceptional defender is back on his game in time for the 2010 tournament.

Years	Caps	Starts	Minutes	Goals	Assists	Yellow	Red
2004–2009	51	50	4,380	5	3	14	2

Chad Marshall

Jonathan Spector

Brian Ching

Jose Francisco Torres

Brad Guzan

Benny Feilhaber

DaMarcus Beasley

Head Coach Bob Bradley

Managing a national soccer team is one of the more thankless jobs in the world. With few sides able to maintain long-term lineup stability, the head coach inevitably becomes a lightning rod for criticism because he is often the only person on the field (or sideline, at least) for every game a country plays. His is a challenging job in this modern era of soccer, with players competing in countries all over the globe, heavy club schedules leading to inevitable injuries, and high salaries making many players difficult to coach. It's not surprising that few national coaches last more than a single World Cup cycle.

It was against this backdrop that Bob Bradley became the latest coach of the United States Men's National Team. He was anything but a high-profile hire—in fact his move into the position looked a lot more like the USSF sneaking Bradley into a side door.

Bradley was preceded in the position by a legend, Bruce Arena, arguably the most successful national coach in U.S. history. Arena coached the team for eight years, including during the successful 2002 World Cup, but his contract was not renewed after the disappointing 2006 World Cup. Many speculated that the USSF would make a splashy hire.

California transplant Jurgen Klinsmann—most recently Germany's coach—was the person most frequently linked to the opening. But the marriage with Klinsmann never came to pass and months went by while the job stayed vacant.

Then in December 2006, there was a development that would ultimately prove a key to the U.S. team's quest for a spot in South Africa: U.S. Soccer quietly named Bob Bradley as the team's interim coach. Bradley, a former MLS coach of the year with the Chicago Fire, clearly had a resume to support his candidacy for the job. Most recently he had been a U.S. assistant in charge of the U.S. Under-23 squad, but many considered him a coach for the future whose chance for the permanent head job would probably come a World Cup cycle or two down the road.

Bob Bradley spent nine seasons as a head coach in MLS before being named Men's National Team coach following the disappointment of the 2006 World Cup. Though initially tagged with the "interim" label, Bradley quickly seized the reins and made the job his own.

Bradley quickly shrugged off the "runner up" labeled and ably regrouped the national team in early 2007. When the team responded positively to his coaching style and delivered quality victories in friendlies against Mexico and Denmark, Bradley's interim tag was removed in May of that year. Since taking over the job, he has compiled a solid 34–16–6 record. More importantly, he has inspired the team to deliver victories at times when it has most needed them, and he kept the squad focused as it successfully negotiated a difficult qualifying tournament for the 2010 World Cup.

Born in Montclair, New Jersey, and a 1980 graduate of Princeton, Bradley is very much a product of the American soccer culture. He became a college head coach (for Ohio University) at the age of 22, then was an assistant for Bruce Arena at Virginia before moving to his alma mater as head coach. Bradley coached Princeton for 12 seasons, leading the team to its only Final Four appearance, before he again became an assistant to Bruce Arena—this time with D.C. United in Major League Soccer's inaugural season. Bradley went on to be the head coach for three different MLS clubs (MetroStars and Chivas USA in addition to the Fire) before responding to the call to work with the U.S. national team.

Part of Bradley's success comes from an aggressive mindset when it comes to scheduling: he looks to take on the best teams the world has to offer to expose his players to elite competition.

The History of the
U.S. Men's National Team

The Early Years

While fans are excited with the recent performance of the United States Men's National Team—2010 will mark its sixth straight appearance in the finals—there is a bit of a misconception that soccer is a new sport in the U.S. Admittedly, American World Cup performance often left much to be desired prior to 1990, but soccer and the Men's National Team have a long history in the U.S.

Soccer originated in England, and soccer-like games were played in the British North American colonies as far back as the 1600s. Some semblance of organization was imported from England in the middle of the 19th century. The Boston-based Oneida club, dating to 1862, was likely the first formal soccer team in the U.S.

In 1884, the first national soccer organization was formed—the American Football Association. It sponsored its first competition, the American Cup, in 1885 and organized a national team that played two games against Canada. The first, in November 1885, was won by Canada 1–0, but the U.S. prevailed 3–2 in a rematch the following year.

Despite this promising start, the AFA never established itself as a truly national organization.

When competitive international soccer was formally launched with the 1904 creation of FIFA, the U.S. initially was not included. This finally changed with the creation of the U.S. Football Association (later renamed U.S. Soccer Federation), giving the United States full membership in FIFA in 1914.

Two years later, the U.S. formed its first official national team, which debuted with a trip to Scandinavia. In its first sanctioned international match, in Stockholm on August 20, 1916, the U.S. Men's National Team defeated Sweden 3–2.

The 1920s are considered soccer's glory era in this country. The first professional league—the American Professional Soccer League—was formed in 1921, centered in the Northeast. Matches regularly drew 10,000 or more fans, roughly the same attendance as NFL games in the same era.

The United States played in three of the first four World Cups, 1930, 1934, and 1950, failing to qualify only in 1938. (No tournament was held in 1942 or 1946 because of World War II and its impacts.) In 1930, the U.S. finished third—still the highest placing in the tournament for any country outside of Europe or South America.

The United States' third-place finish at the 1930 World Cup remains their best showing in the tournament. They won their group before falling to Argentina in the semifinals.

The Modern Era

After qualifying for the 1950 World Cup, the U.S. national team seemingly went into a four-decade-long hibernation. During this time, soccer found itself falling behind other American team sports that were building ever-larger followings. The North American Soccer League, which lasted from 1967 to 1985, enjoyed some success, especially in the 1970s, but it built its following primarily by importing aging stars from overseas: Pele, Giorgio Chinaglia, and Karl-Heinz Granitza among others.

Meanwhile, the national team unraveled into a poorly organized, part-time effort. The U.S. team hit bottom in 1986 with a particularly poor performance during the World Cup qualifying round. Coming on the heels of the NASL shutdown, this failure suggested that the end was near for soccer in the U.S. Instead, an amazing rebirth was just around the corner.

In 1987 the U.S. Soccer Federation became convinced that hosting a World Cup was the only viable solution for salvaging the sport's flagging fortunes and started an all-out effort to secure the 1994 tournament. Some considered the bid ludicrous. Others pointed out that the United States possessed the organizational skills, financing, and infrastructure necessary to host an event of this size. The optimists won out, and in 1988 the U.S. was awarded the tournament.

In 1989 the U.S. team unexpectedly qualified for the 1990 World Cup. With the U.S. facing likely elimination on the road against favored Trinidad & Tobago, American Paul Cagliuri launched a 35-yard rocket into the net to give the U.S. a 1–0 victory and a trip to Italy.

Though the Americans left the 1990 Cup without a win, their mere presence gave momentum to the unfolding drama at home. In 1991 Bora Milutinovic was hired as coach, and the U.S. team became more of a professional endeavor—complete with player contracts, regular practice, and numerous games against quality opponents—on par with the rest of the world. They were ready to play host.

Soccer aficionados from around the globe look back fondly on 1994—it is thought by many to be the best-run, most successful World Cup of all time. Nearly 3.6 million fans attended matches in venues across the country. On the pitch, the U.S. played well and advanced to the second round before falling to eventual champion Brazil.

The 1994 World Cup marked the official return of the U.S. to the national stage, but more importantly it fueled a rebirth of soccer at home. The U.S. made good on its promise (a condition demanded by FIFA on awarding the 1994 Cup) of launching a new national professional league—Major League Soccer, in 1996. MLS is still going strong and helping create a whole new generation of soccer fans.

As the United States prepares to compete in its ninth World Cup, the country finds itself in a very different position from its first Cup of the "modern era" 20 years ago. When a country has been to six

straight tournaments, has players competing in the world's top professional leagues, and has one of the best national organizations, just qualifying isn't reward enough. In October 2009, USSF President Sunil Gulati surprised many people when he told the press that the U.S. was good enough to win in 2010. "I'm deadly serious. Why would we bother going if we didn't think we could win it?"

1990 World Cup

Coach Bob Gansler traveled to Italy with a relatively inexperienced squad comprised of players little known outside the U.S. The team opened the tournament tentatively, losing 5–1 to Czechoslovakia, but rebounded with a solid performance in losing 1–0 to Italy (the eventual champion). The Americans' first World Cup experience in 40 years ended with a third loss—2–1 to Austria—but there was hope for the future.

1994 World Cup

With the United States hosting the tournament for the first time, pressure was on the home team to play like it deserved to be part of soccer's world championship. The U.S. opened the tournament with a 1–1 draw against Switzerland in the Pontiac

Eric Wynalda is challenged by a trio of Columbians during the United States' shocking 2–1 victory over the South American power in the 1994 World Cup.

(Detroit) Silverdome, the first World Cup game played indoors. The Americans followed up with a stunning 2–1 upset of pre-tournament favorite Columbia and a 1–0 loss to Romania, but their four points was enough to push them into the Round of 16. In the knockout phase, the Americans lost 1–0 to eventual champion Brazil but gave good account of themselves in a physical match.

1998 World Cup

The tournament in France was a huge disappointment for the U.S. and marked by controversy. Coach Steve Sampson shocked the country by leaving midfielder John Harkes—whom he had recently named "captain for life"—at home. The turmoil undermined squad unity, key players Eric Wynalda and Tab Ramos were slowed by injuries, and the team responded with three losses in the group stage: 2–0 to Germany, 2–1 to Iran, and 1–0 to Yugoslavia. Based on zero points and the minus-4 goal differential, the U.S. finished dead last in the 32-team tournament, and Sampson resigned days after the last game.

2002 World Cup

The 2002 World Cup, hosted jointly by Japan and South Korea, proved a watershed event for the U.S. team. New coach Bruce Arena assembled a talented squad infused with ample young talent, notably DaMarcus Beasley and Landon Donovan. In its opening Group D match, the U.S. team defeated heavily favored Portugal 3–2. A 1–1 draw with South Korea and a 3–1 loss to Poland left the U.S. with four points, enough to advance to the Round of 16. Waiting was rival Mexico, but Donovan and Brian McBride scored as the U.S. moved on to the quarterfinals with a convincing 2–0 victory. The tournament ended for the Americans with a hard-fought 1–0 loss to Germany, but they proved that they had indeed moved back into the upper tier of world soccer.

2006 World Cup

Expectations for Bruce Arena's second World Cup team were extremely high...then the tournament draw was announced, and the air came out of the balloon. The U.S. found itself in the "group of death" with Italy, the Czech Republic, and Ghana. The Americans came out flat in their first game and dropped a 3–1 decision to the Czechs. The second match, a veritable bloodbath against eventual champion Italy in which three red cards were issued, ended in a 1–1 draw. Needing a victory over Ghana to advance, the Americans were outplayed by the Africans and bowed out of the tournament with a 2–1 loss. The loss prompted the USSF not to renew the contract of Bruce Arena. He ended his successful eight-year run as coach with the most wins in U.S. history, 71.

Landon Donovan was a star of the 2002 World Cup team that launched the U.S. into the upper echelon of world soccer. His goal in the round of 16 victory over Mexico helped propel the Americans into the quarterfinals.

Retired World Cup Stars
1990-2006

The following listing is far from complete, but it highlights several of the players who led America's resurgence as a global soccer power starting with the 1990 World Cup.

Jeff Agoos

Position: Defender

U.S. MNT: 1988–2003

Caps: 104 • Goals: 4

World Cups (2): 1998, 2002

Inducted into National Soccer Hall of Fame: 2009

Born in Switzerland as the son of a U.S. diplomat, Jeff Agoos moved to Texas as a child, played soccer for the University of Virginia, and was one of the top defenders for the U.S. Men's National Team in the 1990s. Despite playing a key role in World Cup qualifiers and major tournaments for much of that decade, he did not play for the U.S. in a World Cup game until 2002—and is best remembered in that competition for an own goal and a tournament-ending injury in the third game. Agoos was on the 1998 squad but stayed on the bench for all three games. He was also the last player cut from the 1994 squad and was so frustrated by the snub that he burned his national team uniform. He was much more successful on the club level, playing in the MLS from the league's inception, winning five championships (two with San Jose, three with D.C. United), and being named MLS Defender of the Year in 2001. Agoos retired in 2005 following a single season playing for the MetroStars and later joined the management team of the New York Red Bulls.

Marcelo Balboa

Position: Defender

U.S. MNT: 1988–2000

Caps: 128 • Goals: 13

World Cups (3): 1990, 1994, 1998

Inducted into National Soccer Hall of Fame: 2005

Born in Chicago and raised in California by Argentine parents (his father played soccer professionally in Argentina and in the NASL), Marcelo Balboa was the first U.S. player to earn 100 caps, a feat he accomplished in 1995. Recognized for his long, flowing locks, he also merits consideration as the greatest defender in U.S. history. He made his first international appearance in 1988, eventually became captain of the U.S. men's team, and was one of three players (along with Tab Ramos and Eric Wynalda) to appear in the '90, '94, and '98 World Cups. He was named USA Male

Known for his flashy play—and his signature bicycle kicks—Marcelo Balboa was one of the most well-known faces of the Men's National Team throughout the 1990s and was named to MLS' All-Time Best XI.

Soccer Athlete of the Year twice—in 1992 and 1994. On the club level, Balboa played in the American Professional Soccer League, moved to Mexico (Leon) for two seasons, then returned to the U.S. with the start of MLS. He played six seasons for the Colorado Rapids, leading the team to the MLS Cup in 1997, and retired in 2002 after a single injury-plagued season with the MetroStars. In the years since, Balboa has been a television analyst for soccer broadcasts on ABC, ESPN, and NBC.

Paul Caligiuri

Position: Defender/Defensive Midfielder

U.S. MNT: 1984–1997

Caps: 110 • Goals: 5

World Cups (2): 1990, 1994

Inducted into National Soccer Hall of Fame: 2004

Despite toiling for years in a defensive role, Paul Caligiuri is best remembered for two goals. The first—against Trinidad & Tobago in a 1989 World Cup qualifier—has been dubbed the "shot heard round the world." It gave the United States a 1–0 victory and its first berth in the Cup finals in 40 years. The second goal—scored in a 5–1 drubbing at the hands of Czechoslovakia at the 1990 World Cup—was the first Cup goal for the Americans since 1950. A California native, Caligiuri starred at UCLA but was a rare American (in that era) to make his mark on the club level in Europe, playing for four different teams in the German Bundesliga. He returned to the States with the launch of MLS, playing one season in Columbus

and five with the L.A. Galaxy. He retired after the 2001 campaign after logging time in 135 MLS matches. Since the end of his playing days, Caligiuri has coached—first on the college level at Cal Poly Pomona (both men and women) and

more recently on the youth level.

Thomas Dooley

Position: Defender/Defensive Midfielder

U.S. MNT: 1992–1998

Caps: 81 • Goals: 7

World Cups (2): 1994, 1998

Inducted into National Soccer Hall of Fame: 2010

Thomas Dooley's journey to stardom on the United States Men's National Team was an unusual one. His father was an American serviceman, his mother was German, and he grew up in Germany. He was in the midst of a solid career as a professional soccer player in the

Paul Caligiuri started every game for the United States in the 1990 and 1994 World Cups and spent several years in the 1990s on contract to play only for the Men's National Team.

Bundesliga when he was discovered by the U.S. Soccer Federation. In fact, it was after Dooley helped lead Kaiserslautern to the championship in 1990–91 that the USSF realized he held a U.S. dual citizenship and recruited him for the national team. He made his mark immediately. He was named USA Male Soccer Athlete of the Year in 1993 and played every minute of the 1994 World Cup. In 1998 he was named captain after the controversial dismissal of John Harkes. After a long career in Germany, Dooley moved to the U.S. and joined the Columbus Crew in 1997. He retired after four MLS seasons, returned to Germany to coach FC Saarbrucken for two seasons, then moved to California, where he works in youth soccer.

Brad Friedel

Position: Goalkeeper	
U.S. MNT: 1992–2005	
Caps: 82 • Goals: 0	
World Cups (3): 1994, 1998, 2002	

Some soccer pundits have dubbed Brad Friedel the all-time top American goalkeeper, and others have called him the top U.S. soccer player—at any position—of all time. These are stunning accolades, especially considering that he often struggled to get in the net for the U.S. and only ranks third all time for caps earned by a U.S. keeper. Yet this speaks more about the quality of U.S. keepers over that last 20 years (think Tony Meola, Kasey Keller, Tim Howard) than for Friedel's skills, which remain among the best in the world

even though he retired from international competition in 2005. In World Cup play, Friedel backed up Meola in 1994, split time with Keller in 1998, and achieved stardom with a fantastic showing in 2002. On the club level, he bounced from Denmark to Turkey to Columbus of the MLS, where he became a star. Liverpool took notice and swept him over to England, but it was after he transferred to Blackburn in 2000 that he became one of the top goalkeepers in the EPL. Freidel currently is the number-one keeper for Aston Villa, backed up by fellow American Brad Guzan.

While Brad Friedel may be retired from the Men's National Team following three World Cup appearances, he remains a solid fixture in soccer. His run of 215 straight appearances in the English Premiership is a record that gets added to every time he takes the pitch.

John Harkes

Position: Midfielder	
U.S. MNT: 1987–2000	
Caps: 90 • Goals: 6	
World Cups (2): 1990, 1994	
Inducted into National Soccer Hall of Fame: 2005	

John Harkes merits consideration as one of the greatest American soccer players of all time, but he is best remembered for being cut from the U.S. squad prior to the disastrous 1998 World Cup. Coach Steve Sampson made the stunning move despite previously naming Harkes "captain for life"—and the fact that he might have been the best player on the team. His otherwise superlative career included solid showings at both the 1990 and 1994 World Cups. Harkes played for the University of Virginia then moved to England to play for Sheffield Wednesday starting in 1990. That season was marked by him scoring England's "goal of the year," becoming the second American to score a goal at venerable Wembley Stadium (during the League Cup final), and helping Wednesday earn a promotion to the First Division—a move that made Harkes the first American to play in what is now known as the EPL. Harkes stayed in England until the launch of MLS in 1996. He led D.C. United to MLS Cup titles in the league's first two seasons and played for New England and Columbus before retiring in 2002. He has remained a fixture in soccer as the lead soccer analyst for ESPN/ABC.

Cobi Jones

Position: Midfielder	
U.S. MNT: 1992–2004	
Caps: 164 • Goals: 15	
World Cups (3): 1994, 1998, 2002	

No player has made more appearances for the United States Men's National Team than Cobi Jones, and few are remembered as fondly. With his blazing speed and distinctive dreadlocks, Jones injected the 1990s-era American team with both energy and personality. He was a sparkplug in two games at the 1994 World Cup and a mainstay in the 1998 tournament, in which he played every minute. Jones was born in Detroit but grew up in southern California, and he will always be associated with California soccer. He starred at UCLA after joining the team as a walk-on, played short stints for professional clubs in England and Brazil, and returned home to L.A. to join the Galaxy for the start of MLS. He stayed with the club for the rest of his career, retiring in 2007 after playing 305 games, scoring 70 goals, and playing in five All-Star games. Since 2008, Jones has served as a Galaxy assistant coach on the staff of former U.S. head man Bruce Arena.

(above) The first American to play in the English Premier League, midfielder John Harkes was a key contributor on the 1990 and 1994 World Cup squads. (opposite) The all-time leader in caps for the United States, Cobi Jones' distinctive style and hard, consistent play won him fans all over the world.

Kasey Kellar

Position: Goalkeeper

U.S. MNT: 1990–2007

Caps: 102 • Goals: 0

World Cups (4): 1990, 1998, 2002, 2006

Over the past 20 years, Kasey Keller has been a world-class goalkeeper, but he has had the misfortune of playing during an era in which the U.S. has been blessed with extraordinary talent in the net. Though he first played for the American team in 1990 and excelled on the club level in Europe starting in 1992, he was left off the U.S. squad in 1994, split time with Brad Friedel in 1998, and sat on the bench behind Friedel in 2002. Keller finally got the

nod in 2006, and though the U.S. underachieved, he was named Man of the Match after the physical 1–1 draw with Italy. Professionally, Keller has played primarily in England, but he also enjoyed stints in Spain and Germany. In 2009 he returned to his native Washington to play for the expansion Seattle Sounders and set an MLS record for most minutes to start a season without giving up a goal—457.

Alexei Lalas

Position: Defender

U.S. MNT: 1991–1998

Caps: 96 • Goals: 9

World Cups (2): 1994, 1998

Inducted into National Soccer Hall of Fame: 2006

Thanks to his big shock of red hair, long red goatee, and rock 'n' roll attitude, Alexei Lalas was warmly embraced by American soccer fans. It also didn't hurt that he played four solid games during the 1994 World Cup and was recognized as an honorable mention All-Star after the tournament. Though his time as a marquee-quality player was short compared to most of the others in this section, Lalas' impact on American soccer is undeniable. After growing up in Michigan and playing in college for Rutgers, Lalas found himself playing in Italy's Serie A for Padova. He came back to the United States with the start of MLS in 1996 and joined the New England Revolution. He also played for the MetroStars and Kansas City before

(above) No United States goalkeeper has started more games or kept more clean sheets than Kasey Keller. His fine form with the Seattle Sounders has shown that despite his retirement from the international game, Keller is still an elite keeper. (opposite) The first American in the modern era to take his game to Italy's Serie A, Alexi Lalas remains one of the most visible figures in United States soccer nearly seven years after he last laced up his boots.

finishing up his career with the L.A. Galaxy. Smart and personable, Lalas was a natural candidate for MLS management and ended up serving as general manager for San Jose, the MetroStars, and the Galaxy—with mixed success. After getting fired by L.A., Lalas turned to broadcasting and serves as a studio analyst for ABC/ESPN.

Brian McBride

Position: Forward

U.S. MNT: 1993–2006

Caps: 96 • Goals: 30

World Cups (3): 1998, 2002, 2006

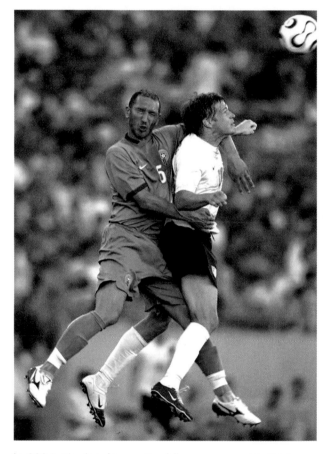

A masterful scorer with his head and maybe the top American player in English Premiership League history, Brian McBride may be best known as one of the hardest-working U.S. players of all time. He is also the only U.S. player to have scored goals in more than one World Cup—he netted the ball in both 1998 and 2002, including two game-winners in the latter tournament. He didn't score in 2006, but he will be long remembered for staying in the game against Italy despite getting an elbow to the face that left him bloodied and needing stitches. On the club level, McBride played a short stint in Germany before returning for the MLS debut in 1996. He became a star during eight seasons with Columbus Crew but couldn't resist a call to Fulham in England in 2004. Playing for parts of five seasons, McBride scored 40 goals, was named captain, and became arguably the team's most valuable and most popular player—a battler who worked hard and wasn't afraid to get physical. In 2008 he returned home to play for the Chicago Fire and continued his goal-scoring ways, though his 2009 season was cut short by a shoulder injury.

A star in England and in MLS as well as one of the greatest U.S. players of all time, Brian McBride was a goal-scoring terror with his head. He is the only American player with a goal in two different World Cups.

Claudio Reyna

Position: Midfielder

U.S. MNT: 1994–2006

Caps: 112 • Goals: 8

World Cups (4): 1994, 1998, 2002, 2006

"Captain America" (as he was called by the British press) Claudio Reyna was dogged by injuries throughout his long career, but when he was healthy he could fairly be included among the world's elite players. He played professionally in three top-level European leagues and he was on the roster for four different World Cups (as well as captain of the 2002 and 2006 teams)—credentials that place him among America's all-time greats. Born and raised in New Jersey to Argentine parents (his father had been a professional soccer player), Reyna attended the same high school that produced Tab Ramos. He played three seasons for Virginia then jumped to the German Bundesliga, where he played for Bayer Leverkusen and VfL Wolfsburg. Before finishing up his career in MLS with the New York Red Bulls, Reyna played in Scotland (Rangers) and England (Sunderland and Manchester City). On the international stage, injuries kept Reyna off the pitch during the 1994 World Cup, but in 2002 he became only the second American to be named to the all-tournament team. He followed that up with another solid tournament in 2006, after which he retired from the U.S. team.

Eric Wynalda

Position: Forward

U.S. MNT: 1990–2000

Caps: 107 • Goals: 34

World Cups (3): 1990, 1994, 1998

Inducted into National Soccer Hall of Fame: 2004

Until he was passed by Landon Donovan in 2008, Eric Wynalda was the all-time leading scorer for the U.S. MNT—status he earned while becoming one of only three Americans to play in three straight World Cups. He also scored Major League Soccer's first goal, in 1996 while playing for the San Jose Clash. On the other hand, the temperamental Wynalda also has the dubious distinction of the first American to be red-carded in a World Cup game (against Czechoslovakia in 1990) and was infamous for conflicts with coaches throughout his career. The California native played for San Diego State and sporadically for the APSL San Francisco Blackhawks while focusing his efforts on the U.S. national team. In 1992 Wynalda joined German club Saarbrucken and became the first American to play in the top division of the Bundesliga. Four years later, he was on hand for the start of MLS. He played for four different clubs before injuries ended his career in 2001. Currently, he is a broadcaster for FSC and recently played (briefly) for lowly Bakersfield of the USL Premier Development League.

TRIUMPH
BOOKS